Adventures of a South Dakota Kid

Bert Moritz

12/19/16

To LaVonne —
A wonderful patient
and a wonderful life!

Your Friend,

Bert Moritz

First published by Dog Ear Publishing
4011 Vincennes Rd
Indianapolis, IN 46268
www.dogearpublishing.net

ISBN: 978-1-4575-4553-5

This book is printed on acid-free paper.

Printed in the United States of America

To
Susan Emeline Quigley Moritz.
Thank you for being so special!

Contents

Introduction

My name is Norbert Frank Moritz. Norbert is not a name that I especially like. It's my father's name, and my mother claims she was in the fog post delivery when it was assigned to me. She split the name and called him "Norb" and me "Bert." I don't especially like Bert either, but there it is. I like to think of myself as a storyteller, and this is a collection of stories from my life. They are true, at least as true as memory allows. I don't want you to think this is a history of my life, for that's not what I set out to write. In fact, I didn't set out to write any of this!

A bit of explanation is in order. I write a column for a local senior-citizens' newspaper. It began as a way to teach the public about eye disease, but no one, as far as I could tell, read the darned thing! After eighteen months of creating droll articles with titles such as "Dry Eye" or "Do Your Eyes Itch?" I was asked by the editor to write a column concerning my father. You see, my dad had suffered Alzheimer's disease, and Alzheimer's Awareness Month was coming up. It seemed logical to me that the editor wanted a timely article to spice up the next issue a bit, but it never occurred to me that she was gently suggesting that my eye-disease topics were not engaging her readers.

The next month, patient after patient came into my office commenting on the Alzheimer's article. I was stunned! Had my previous stuff really been that bad? Now, I may be a bit slow on the uptake, but it didn't take a genius to figure out that a change in direction was needed! As a result, my column morphed from being about eye disease to human interest. No longer would I have to describe the medical wonders of Scheme's canal as it relates to facility of outflow in glaucoma, but I could actually choose entertaining topics to my liking. What a relief!

So, the topics contained herein are about my experiences and me. After all, that's what I know best. Despite the particulars of my experiences, I think you'll find the stories are in some way actually about each of us as individuals. We each grow up following much the same pattern, having similar life experiences and sharing similar victories and failures. It is my hope that you can identify with these stories and enjoy remembering your past as much as I have enjoyed experiencing mine!

I was born in 1952 on the plains of mid-America. My grandparents started farming with horses, my parents grew up during the Great Depression, and my generation experienced Vietnam and the space race. I would like to think of myself as exceptional. Unfortunately, I am not exceptionally smart, especially good-looking or even a little rich. I am fortunate to have a good memory and a curiosity about life. Finally, I've found sharing memories with the people who are most important to me to be tremendously rewarding.

I have had a variety of jobs. The present is as optometrist. I wonder what you visualize when you hear the word *optometrist*. Remember that Norman Rockwell painting of a chubby, light-skinned, balding eye doctor placing ugly black horn-rimmed spectacles on a reluctant young boy who is defiantly clutching his base-ball glove? But the profession has served me well. Tens of thousands of patients have paraded though my office through the years. I have done more than merely watch humanity age. I have seen in so many of them what I was, what I am, and what I am to become.

Every writer brings a unique perspective to an effort like this. If my perspective is in any way exceptional, it is from having experienced a life of great variety. When you move around as much as I have, you are bound to pick up a few stories. To date, I have had thirty-eight addresses! Those addresses have been more than a bit diverse. They've included gas stations, dorms, barracks, Quonset huts, apartments, and houses. The smallest town I lived in boasted twenty souls, and the largest, four million. I expect to add three more addresses: a condo when it is time to downsize, a nursing home when I'm failing, and finally, the cemetery. That'll be quite enough.

You and I never know when a hidden memory will be called out of hibernation, maybe by a song on the radio or the smell of a particular food. It's as if each memory were stored behind a small door in our brains. The door is locked, but a key is waiting in our future; all we need to do is live our lives, and when the time comes, the memory will be set free. Suddenly, we will be greeted by an unexpected pleasure from the past, one that enriches our present experience. Now, what could be better than that!

This book is organized into seven parts. Each part contains a short introduction followed by a series of essays. The theme of each part is not rigid, and each of the essays can stand on its own. I did not write these in any special order, and they are certainly not presented as they happened, so feel free to read them in any order you choose.

Bert Moritz
Fall Creek, Wisconsin
November 2015

Part One—Getting Started

It's been said that there are only two guarantees in life—death and taxes; however, I'm going to take liberty by adding a third, one that we have all had to endure: growing up. We may all have survived it, but not without some bumps and bruises along the way. This section will highlight a few of the pains and milestones I experienced while growing up.

I hope reading these stories will remind you of the pitfalls of maturing. Struggles are guaranteed while learning about the opposite sex, interacting with siblings, and getting into trouble through poor judgment. My parents raised five children, and I still wonder how they managed to guide us all through that difficult phase!

You will, however, also read about many positive experiences I had while maturing. These include buying my first car, enjoying childhood hobbies, and getting a job. You can judge for yourself whether each of these milestones had a positive or a negative effect on me. We can all look back on our lives and speculate how differently we would now be if we could do it all over again. Unfortunately, there is no second chance, and there is no denying that you and I became the adults we are because of the experiences we had while growing up. Let's have a look at one man's experiences, shall we?

Looking for Girls

Growing up is hard, no matter where or how you are raised. Getting that first date was especially traumatic for me. That's not to say that I was socially inept, but realize where I was coming from: My haircuts started out with my mom using dog shears to give me a buzz cut until I graduated to the bowl method. And just at the time when blue jeans were becoming fashionable, I still wore pants and shirts that Mom made on her Singer sewing machine at home. She favored polyester plaid prints.

When I was fifteen years old and my brother Dave was seventeen, we decided one warm summer afternoon that it was time to go looking for girls. Let me tell you, that was a misadventure that we will never forget! Two wild and crazy guys, headed down the road, looking for...

We were living in the small Iowa town of Estherville. The local kids nicknamed it Everstill because there wasn't much to do. About twenty miles away, however, near some lakes, was an amusement park that was open in the summer. Dave and I wanted to go to the park, but we were too embarrassed to let Dad know that we were hoping to meet some girls there, so we hatched a scheme. We'd pretend that we were going fishing but would instead sneak over to the amusement park. So, we put on our church clothes, stuffed ten dollars into our pockets, and set our fishing poles in the backseat of Dad's big old Ford Fairlane. He may have been suspicious when we announced that we were going to Center Lake to catch some crappies, but he didn't question our fishing attire.

Dave decided that we would first drive around Center Lake so we technically could say that we had been there. Just as we came around the far side of the lake, Dave stopped the car. Right there, in our way, was a large barricade erected by a work crew. The sign said, ROAD CLOSED. Beyond the barrier, we could see that the gravel road was a torn-up muddy quagmire from recent construction and heavy rains. The entrance to the park lay just beyond the end of the construction zone.

Now this is the point where common sense should have prevailed, but remember, we were looking for girls and desperation more aptly described our frame of mind! "Maybe we should turn around," my brother said. "The road looks pretty rough."

"Ah, you can make it!" I egged him on. "Let's just drive around those barriers. We are almost there!" So Dave put that big car in gear and he hit the gas! We were moving pretty well at first, but the farther we got, the deeper the mud became. I can remember looking over my shoulder and seeing a black rooster tail shooting out from each spinning back tire! When we had sunk so far that the mud began to pile up over the front bumper, we started going sideways! That beast of a car slid halfway into the ditch and came to a complete stop!

Just getting out of the car was a chore! The mud was up against the doors, and we had to push really hard to open them. Standing in our Sunday shoes, nearly knee-deep in muck, we could see that it was hopeless. We were going to need a tow truck. We looked up. There at the barrier was the county sheriff's car and the construction boss! Boy, did that boss chew Dave out, beginning as soon as we were within shouting distance! A tow truck mercifully arrived to pull Dad's car out, so we each had to cough up our ten-dollar bill to pay for the job. There we stood within eyesight of the park, humiliated, flat broke, and covered in mud! We got back in the car and drove home.

The first thing we did in town was go to a car wash and hose each other off. Next, we cleaned up the car, and then we drove home. After hanging our fishing rods in the garage, we walked past Dad. He looked up from his newspaper and asked us if we had caught any fish. We said, "No!" and kept on walking. He didn't seem to notice that we were soaking wet! Instead, he went back to reading his newspaper. Whew, was I grateful that we had gotten away with that one!

Some years later, after my stint in the Army, I was talking to Dad about growing up. When I started to tell him about the car in the mud, he stopped me. "I know all about that one, Bert. The county cop used the license plate, and he called me before you boys got home. You two could have dried off a bit more before you came into the house." Hearing Dad say that was another reminder that growing up is hard! Just one more bite of humble pie that I had to eat!

Learning to Drive

When I turned fifteen, I knew the time had come to learn to drive a car. Boy, was I excited! I envisioned having my own car. I wouldn't have to bum rides from my older sister and could stop riding my bicycle to high school. And hey, maybe I might even ask a girl out and go on a first date! I was confident that I could master the rules of the road easily. You see, when I was younger, my grandfather out in South Dakota had let me drive his old Plymouth around town. It had a "three on the tree" with a clutch, so it was a jerky ride. There were only one hundred people in town and not a single stop sign, but I hadn't hit anything, so I knew that I was a good driver at a young age.

After signing up for after-school driving instructions, I took my turn driving with the shop teacher. I noticed that he held onto the door handles tightly as I went around corners. When we practiced passing other cars on the highway, he reached over and grabbed the wheel. That didn't bother me because I knew that old people were easily scared. When the class was over, I knew that I had this "safe driving" thing down pat! The next step was to get in some hours driving with my dad in the car.

"No!" My father had always been a man of few words, and he needed only one word when I asked him to ride in the car with me at the wheel. In retrospect, I probably wasn't the best kid on the planet. After all, I had shot my younger brother in the foot with my BB gun, built a bazooka to shoot the city water tower, made gunpowder and put my friend Sam in the hospital twice, exploded hydrogen in our basement... On the list goes. Maybe I hadn't always used good judgment, but nobody's perfect! The old man refused to budge on this one. When I asked, "Why not?" he just looked at me and shook his head. I was going to have to ask my mother.

I really didn't want to ride around with Mom. To be honest, I was embarrassed to ride in the car with her. She was the shortest person I knew. Our car was a big old Dodge, and Mom could not see over the dashboard. She had to sit on a book with a pillow on top of it, and even then, she had to peek under the rim of the steering wheel! I was a bit concerned that she might follow Dad's lead and deny me also. Luckily, I was her favorite child. I wondered if it could be because I was the well-adjusted middle child. When I asked, she agreed to move her book and pillow over to the passenger side while I practiced driving.

Mom wasn't the best instructor. I can remember when she first got her driver's license as an adult. She had felt so liberated that she had begun to smoke a pipe around my father just to let him know how independent she had become! The truth was, however, that Mom drove only in small towns and on uncrowded streets. My lessons with Mom went reasonably well—that is, until it came time to practice parallel parking. She had never actually parallel-parked a car and thought it would be best if I practiced without any other cars in the way. She said that I should just pretend there were nearby cars and go through the motions. We did this over and over. I became quite proficient parking this way, and soon, Mom "graduated" me. I was ready to get my license!

It wasn't especially comfortable sitting in that big old Dodge with a state trooper next to me. The ceiling was so high that he kept his Smokey the Bear hat on. I knew that parallel parking was the last thing I would have to do. Imagine my surprise when we turned back toward the police station and right in front were two parked patrol cars with space in between them. To make matters worse, two girls from my high school class were standing there waiting to be tested after me!

It's really a lot harder to parallel park when there are real cars in the way! I put the transmission into reverse and cranked the wheel hard to the right. I did the best that I could, but the rear bumper ended up flat against the curb and the car's front was pointed straight out into the street! Well, that trooper handed me a rejection slip and gave me some advice: "You had better get your dad to teach you how to parallel park, and don't come back until you are ready." Clearly, it hadn't been the sweat dripping into my eyes or nervousness in front of those girls that had caused me to fail. Here I'd thought that I was such a hotshot driver, and I guess I had just paid the price! Now I was going to have to put my tail between my legs and ask Dad for help again.

My uncle Chuck once told me that life is one long lesson in humility. It's been forty-six years since I got my first driver's license. I have driven oversized military vehicles, railroad locomotives, trucks, Chicago city buses, and more cars than I can remember. I'd like to say that parallel parking is a snap, but I still wish those other cars were not really there!

Ghosts of Christmas Past

Our childhood memories of Christmas are often tainted with feelings about gifts that we may or may not have received. I suppose this is normal. Even today, I get excited before I open a well-wrapped present. If I am disappointed, it is not because the gift is inadequate but because I've created an excessive expectation. When I recall Christmas experiences, a most disappointing one stands out the most. I'll tell you about it, but first ... some fun ones!

One thing about the gifts we kids got is that they were pretty much based on needs, not wants! Our toughest Christmas was when we were living on the farm. Members of the local church knew that we were having financial trouble, so they gave our family gifts. My sister got a doll, the boys each got a white shirt, and

Mom was given a frying pan. Uncle Larry came to the house dressed up as Santa Claus; I have a mid-fifties photograph of me on his lap. I'm holding a brown paper bag full of candy, and my mouth is so full that I look like a chipmunk!

After we moved to a small town in Iowa, I noticed a trend for our holiday presents—why, winter coats, of course! Then family gift-giving moved into a new phase—musical instruments! First, our parents bought our oldest sister a used cornet. Then as each of us kids grew, the cornet was handed down to the next one. The older sibling giving up the cornet was then given a new Sears and Roebuck trumpet. In the end, we had four trumpets and a cornet. Too bad we didn't capitalize and go on TV as a quintet!

So far from what you've read about my childhood, you have probably come to realize that I did get into a lot of trouble! Let's face it: Exploding rockets, bottles of hydrogen, and homemade gunpowder were just a few of the things that got me some well-deserved reprimands! Right now, I'd like to tell you about a mis-adventure that had implications for my most disappointing Christmas.

It all started with my BB gun. Dad gave me a Daisy pump-action rifle on my eleventh birthday. He told me that I had to be responsible. At first, things went along pretty well. I practiced and became a pretty good shooter. To prove that I was using good judgment, I even limited myself to shooting out the windows of only those buildings I thought were abandoned!

Then one day, friend Roy and I were out in the woods. We started speculating about how much it might hurt if we shot each other. Pretty soon, we were engaged in a BB gun war! Unfortunately for Roy, my rifle pumped up pretty well and I shot a BB into the right side of his head, just above his eye. He went off bawling to his mom! Luckily, I was able to convince him to lie and say it had been an accident. When my mother got the phone call from Roy's mom, I was given a stern warning, but I got to keep my gun.

Later that summer, on a hot August day, my younger brother, Paul, and I were in the backyard. I was twelve then, and he was seven. He must have said something that made me angry, so I walked right up to him, put the end of my BB gun on the top of his tennis shoe, and pulled the trigger! He gave out a holler that I will never forget! That night when Dad came home, Mom told him what I had done. I was terrified! Dad told me to bring him the gun. He didn't say a word as he took it from me, put the barrel on his knee, and bent it completely in half! Then he handed it back to me. I got the message.

Two years later, I decided that it was finally time for me to get a real gun. The previous Christmas, my older brother had gotten a hunting rifle, so I told the folks that I wanted a .22-caliber rifle to hunt rabbits, and I expected it at Christmas. After all, I hadn't had any gun trouble for a couple of years, so I felt I had learned my lesson.

On Christmas morning, there was only one gift under the tree for me. It was a long, thin, heavy box! I was so excited! Sure enough, when I opened it, there was a rifle inside. But it wasn't what I'd wanted. It was another Daisy pump-action BB rifle identical to my old one!

I was sad that Christmas morning, but I had recieved a lesson in humility that I knew I deserved! My mother once told me that I grew up going to the school of hard knocks. Now whenever Christmas comes around, I reflect on the past year. I've learned that Christmas is not so much about getting what you want as about getting what you deserve!

Oh, Brother!

Siblings play an important role in our lives as we grow. They are there to witness our successes and failures, and we rely on them for advice and understanding. That's not to say the arrangement is problem-free, but for better or for worse, we love them and they return the favor.

I grew up with an older sister and an older brother and also a younger sister and a younger brother. Thus, I was the middle, well-adjusted one! But I did have a special relationship with my older brother, Dave. He was only a year ahead of me in school, so we had a lot in common. We were especially compatible because I liked to be in charge and Dave seemed to accept my direction, but being too gullible with me around got Dave into more trouble than he deserved! It's not that I intentionally tried to put him in harm's way, but…

When I was in early grade school, our family rented an old farmhouse just outside of Vinton, Iowa. Out back were a barn and a few outbuildings. The owners kept horses in the barn, including a Shetland pony. Boy, was that a mean little horse! She always tried to bite us or scrape us against a fence if we tried to ride her.

One day, I suggested to Dave that he go for a ride out on the county road. He speculated that we should ask Mom first, but I told him that wasn't necessary. Well, he led the pony onto the road, and then he hopped on, bareback. The pony refused to move. "Give her a kick!" I shouted.

When Dave's heels touched the back of that horse, she bolted like a bullet on fire! Dave came flying off the back with his feet pointed at the sky! The gravel stuck in the back of his head wasn't the worst of his problems. The horse was gone and he had to tell Mom. I stood by with my mouth shut as she demanded to know where he had gotten the "lame brain" idea that he could take the pony. Then Mom took off down the road and retrieved the horse.

Dave and I loved playing around that old hay-filled barn. There were plenty of mice and pigeons that made good targets for his BB gun! One summer day on a hunting expedition, we got too hot and sweaty. I explained to Dave that the barn windows couldn't be opened and that it was too hot for the horses, too. "Maybe one of us should shoot out the barn windows and get some air in here before a horse dies," I suggested.

Well when Dad got home and saw all the glass on the ground, did Dave ever get in trouble again! He wasn't sitting very well at supper that night.

One cool fall day about the time in our lives when Dave and I developed an interest in science, we were paging through the Funk & Wagnalls encyclopedia when we came upon a section about Leonardo da Vinci. The sketches of his inventions, especially the parachute, fascinated us. "We can make a better parachute than that!" I told Dave. "Let's get a blanket and try."

So we snuck a sheet from the closet and tied a piece of rope on each of the four corners. I was starting to have my doubts about the project, so I told Dave to tie the ropes to his belt and then jump off the barn roof. Ever compliant, up he climbed! Standing on the edge, with one of Mom's white sheets trailing behind him, Dave looked down. "Jump!" I shouted. "Jump!" At that instant, the back door of the house opened and Mom came barreling out. "Don't jump!" I chanted. "Don't jump!"

"What is that crazy kid doing up there?" Mom demanded.

I shrugged my shoulders and said, "I don't know, Mom, but at least he has a parachute." That day didn't turn out too well for Dave, either.

You might think that my older brother would have quickly wised up and stopped taking direction from me, but it took a surprisingly long time for that to happen! To this day, we laugh about the things we did together.

We can't help but share our lives with our brothers and sisters. For better or for worse, we are in it together.

Roger and Lena

I think each of us can look back on life and find some person or event that had an indelible effect on us that was unknown at the time, and our lives would be profoundly influenced in ways that we could not have predicted. Let me tell you about two people who jointly had such an effect on me. Their names were Roger and Lena.

When I was fifteen years old, I was not a good high school student. Rather than do homework, I would busy myself with a job that I had taken at an old hotel in the small town of Estherville, Iowa. Each afternoon at about four thirty , I'd arrive from school, put on an apron, stand in front of two large metal sinks, and begin to scrub pots. Now, this was not an especially pleasant chore. The pots would be piled high and covered with sticky or burned food. At the end of a shift, I'd always leave for home soaked from head to foot.

I worked alone, but I was not the only pot scrubber. The daytime scrubber was a mentally handicapped fellow named Roger. He was about forty years old, a bit pudgy, quiet, and pleasant to work with. For whatever reason, he seemed satisfied to stand in front of those sinks and grind away with a metal brush on all those huge pots. Day after day with his hands in the hot, dirty water, he would just bear down and get that nasty job done—and he did an excellent job, at that!

The daytime cook was an older woman named Lena. Lena was short, wiry, and tough as nails. That woman could cook like no one else, but boy, did she have a temper! Her shift overlapped with mine for a few hours each day.

As I did my work, I'd hang each pot on a wall-mounted hook. Then Lena would come and take whatever she needed as she prepared food for the evening. More often than I would like to admit, a few seconds later, that same pot would come flying through the air, bang up against the wall, and splash down into the dirty water in front of me. Then Lena would begin her speech about how good a pot scrubber Roger was and how bad I was.

One especially hot afternoon, I picked up a heavy pot that Lena had just thrown back in my direction. Studying it carefully, I could see the burned and dried food that had caused her consternation. It suddenly occurred to me that maybe Lena was right—Roger was not only a better pot scrubber than I was but was a better pot scrubber than I could ever be. He was built for this kind of work and I just wasn't. If someone were going to be laid off around here, it wouldn't be Roger; it would be me!

It instantly dawned on me that I would have to do something that the Rogers of the world could not do. Standing there in that kitchen, I concluded that I would need to work harder in high school, get my grades up, and then try to get into a college.

A mentally handicapped man and a cranky cook helped to get me pointed in the right direction. Isn't it odd how we can be influenced by someone or something when we least expect it?

The More You Sweat in Time of Peace...

When I was a senior in high school, I decided to go to college. At that time, my father had gotten a promotion on the Rock Island Railroad. His duties included scheduling the trains and hiring and firing work crews. Dad must have figured that it was time that I grow up and earn some real money, for he hired both my older brother and me for summer railroad work. Dave was put on a track crew as a gandy dancer. And me? I was assigned to the car department to be a car toad. I was pretty confident that I could do that job. After all, how hard could it be? Let me tell you...

My shift started at eleven o'clock at night and went until eight o'clock in the morning. I spent the time working by myself in the switchyard, where scores of railroad cars were lined up on eight tracks. The switching crew would be operating an engine, lining up cars for the morning trains. It was dangerous to work around the moving cars in the dark, so I had to avoid the tracks they would be working on.

I had three jobs each night. The first job was to change worn brake shoes on the cars. Each shoe was a twenty-pound cast-iron device. Carrying two in each hand, I walked up and down the tracks. When I spotted a thin or worn-out shoe, I would use a crowbar to pry it away from the steel wheel. This was not easy. Then I'd replace it with a new shoe. More than once, my fingers got caught between the shoe and the wheel!

My second job was to oil the boxes. Each wheel axle had a square metal box on both ends. Inside the box was a large sheepskin pad that provided lubricant to the wheel bearings. Keeping the wheel bearings oiled was mandatory because if they got dry, the axle would heat up and melt the whole assembly. This was called a hot box, and many a train had been derailed through neglect of this job. I would walk the length of each train with a large can filled with heavy-weight oil in one hand and a long metal hook in the other. Using the hook, I'd yank open the box door and pour oil over the pad. Kicking the box shut with my boot, I would move on to the next axle.

My final job started with a hike over to the turntable. There, I had to furnish the locomotives with fuel, water, and sand. Then I had to drive them onto the turntable and line them up according to train orders. These diesel behemoths each weighed one hundred tons!

One night after hooking five engines together, I drove them slowly to the end of the turntable. In my haste, however, I'd forgotten to set the air brakes! You can't imagine the panic in my chest when throwing the break lever had no effect on those engines! All five hundred tons of locomotive just kept rolling toward the end of the track! Fortunately, some smart railroader must have known that a young fool like me would make this mistake. At the end of the turntable was a massive block of steel.

When those five engines hit that block, the resounding boom surely awakened every living soul in town! A bit later, the switching crew came by, chuckling about the incident. I just ignored them.

Halfway through my first summer working for the railroad, Dad assigned me to work the day carman job for vacation relief. I got to ride around in a big truck with two other Carmen, named Chuck and Buck. These men were hardworking, hard-swearing fellas! I needed to pull my weight with these guys, and being the boss's skinny kid did not help one bit.

On my first day out, while driving to a job, Chuck turned off the main road and we stopped at a little cafe for lunch. Chuck explained, "We like to eat off the tracks, away from the boss. A beer can taste pretty good on a hot day like this. What're you going to have to drink?" I knew these guys figured that if they got me to have a beer, then I wouldn't squeal on them for having one.

Not having a beer meant that I would be in for a long summer with them. My decision? Let's just say that my burger and fries went down pretty well that day!

The next time I was confronted with alcohol on the job, it was a bit more complicated. Near the end of my second summer, we had a derailment in the switching yard. Three cars had fallen off the tracks and we had to get them back on as soon as possible. All crews were called in and we worked hard and fast.

About four in the morning, we took a break. Six of us stood in a circle, shooting the breeze. One of the track crew reached into his jacket and pulled out a tin whiskey flask. Opening it up, he took a sip and passed it around. Looking over at me, he snarled, "Don't give any to him. He's Moritz's kid." The man beside me took a hit and then started to hand it to me. Suddenly, an arm snaked in from the dark and snatched the flask right out of his hand! Stepping into the circle was my dad! We all froze! Each of us could be fired, and my dad could do it on the spot.

"Who has the cap?" was all he asked. The track man sent it over. Dad scowled at him and said, "If you want this back, I'll see you in my office." Then he turned and left. We scurried back to work like a bunch of scared rabbits!

My summer railroad job ended abruptly after Richard Nixon sent me a draft notice. Two weeks later, I was doing fifty sit-ups in front of a sign that carried our company motto: "The more you sweat in time of peace, the less you bleed in time of war." With the help of some heavy work and those hard railroaders, however, this scrawny nineteen-year-old kid was ready to take what the Army had to throw at him. I'd learned how to hold my own with other men. Dad's judgment really paid off. Oh, and that tin whiskey flask? It remained on Dad's desk, never to be picked up!

The Vinton Tornado

Extreme circumstances can sometimes thrust us into unexpected situations. We cannot be sure how we'll react in truly novel environments, because we can never be adequately prepared. The results are often unpredictable, sometimes tragic, and occasionally even humorous. I want to tell you how our family reacted when we were nearly blown away by a fierce storm.

After leaving the farm in South Dakota, my father learned Morse code and became a telegrapher for the Rock Island Railroad. His work had brought us to the small town of Vinton, Iowa. There, we rented an old farmhouse on an acreage located well outside of town. Dad would be gone for a week at a time, providing central agency services to other small-town depots. Mom had the sole responsibility of caring for us five kids at an isolated and lonely farmstead. We children ranged in age from one to twelve years.

It was a late Sunday morning in April of 1961. Rather than attending church, we were outdoors, playing around the old barn. Mom had grown up on a farm, knew about bad weather, and didn't like what she saw that morning, so she had decided that we would skip Mass. Outdoors, Dave and I couldn't help but notice the sweltering heat and oppressive humidity. The farmyard was eerily quiet, and what few sounds there were were strangely muffled.

Mom spotted huge gray clouds rolling in from the west. Opening the back door, she yelled out to us, "There's a storm coming! You kids get in the house right now!" I recall sprinting into the front room and standing near the picture window so I could watch the approaching storm.

The sky quickly turned a menacing dark green, and the wind started howling. Then the sound of the wind changed. It was just like the noise of a fast freight train that I had heard in a depot. The trees across the gravel road were slapped to the ground like the hand of a hidden giant had just punched them! Mom started screaming, "It's a tornado! It's a tornado! Get into the cellar now!" She grabbed the baby and came after us as we flew down the steps. Just as she came through the cellar door, we heard a loud blast of breaking glass and felt ice-cold air. Then the lights went out and the wood floor over our heads began to crack. Finally, there was a great explosive boom. Just as suddenly as it had started, the chaos departed, leaving only the pattering of a light rain and our own sobbing and tears.

We climbed the cellar stairs slowly. The house was still there, but boy, what a mess! It looked like... well... it looked like a tornado had gone through it! Every window was blown out, and our furniture and things had been thrown everywhere! The barn was gone, the corncrib was upside down, and the house had been lifted up off its foundation and then dropped back down again! Mom lit a candle and asked us to pray. We stood in the kitchen, trying to decide what to do. At that very moment, my older sister turned to me and blurted out, "There is no Santa Claus. It's Mom and Dad!" I have no idea why she chose that very moment to tell me this, but I do remember looking around the house and thinking that there wasn't going to be a present under the tree for any of us that Christmas.

There was my mom with five scared kids, the house in shambles, and her husband working out of town. To make matters worse, she had just gotten her driver's license and she had never driven our beat-up old Plymouth with a floor shift! She gathered up what she could and loaded the bunch of us into the car. Then she steered for Vinton.

Mom took us to the only hotel in town, and we all went up to the front desk together. Now, we youngsters had never been in a hotel before, so imagine my mom with five not-so-clean kids all huddled around her. The clerk told her that all the rooms were reserved for the incoming utility work crews responding to storm damage. Mom was completely devastated, so she started to cry!

The desk clerk must have felt pretty bad for us. He kindly allowed us to stay the night in the second-floor common sitting room using the couch and a rollaway bed for sleeping arrangements. To this day, I remember walking into the room with my older brother and seeing an old leather chair. We immediately stuck our hands down the edge of the seat cushion and found some coins! Who could imagine people so rich that they had money falling out of their pockets when they sat in that chair?

Thanks to my mom's weather awareness and quick thinking, our family survived the Vinton tornado, but her hard work had just begun. She now had to salvage what was left in the ruined house and move us to another town.

What about Santa Claus? Well, we all have to get that bad news eventually. It just goes to show you that crazy things can happen in unexpected situations!

First Date

Susie and I have been married for thirty-six years. I'm not going to tell you how fast the time has passed or how surprised I am that my next wedding anniversary is just around the corner, but what I will tell you is this: I'm not just surprised that I found the best girl on the planet; I am amazed that I found anyone at all!

You see, when it came to dating; I was anything but smooth, cool, or devil-may-care. In fact, the first time I asked a girl out, I was walking home from school. I went to high school in the small town of Estherville, Iowa. As a freshman, I didn't have a real job yet, so I was still wearing clothes that Mom had sewn for me. My pants were a colorful print that must have been popular in Czechoslovakia at the time, and my red-and-blue shirt was in the same western style that she made for my brothers. Fortunately, I had enough money to go to the barbershop. My days of a butch or bowl haircut by Mom were finally over!

One day while looking ahead on the sidewalk, whom did I see? Why, it was Wanda Watson, the very same girl I had wanted to dance with at the eighth-grade mixer! I could still see her standing across the gym from me. I remembered her straight blonde hair and green dress, and I could still hear the Beatles's tune "Penny Lane" playing in the background. I had stood with my back against the gym wall, staring at Wanda—for the full two hours! Too terrified to dance, I certainly hadn't even tried to talk to her! But now here she was, just a few awkward feet from me. Her football-playing boyfriend with the letter jacket and hot car must not have been around to drive her home from school. This was my big chance to get my first date with the girl of my dreams!

"Oh, hi, Wanda. It's nice to see you. How are you doing?"

"Fine."

Wow! I was actually talking to this girl and it was going pretty well. *Now what do I say?*

"I don't see you here very often. Do you like walking home from school?"

"No."

We're really getting along quite well and I can tell that she likes talking to me. This is going great! The time is right. I need to pop the big question. Go ahead, you can do it!

"Would you like to go on a date with me?"

"No. I don't date guys who have a shiny nose."

Wow! It was like a punch in the gut! My legs were paralyzed, and I just stood there, embarrassed. Wanda walked on by herself. I had never considered my complexion before. My older sister called me "pizza face" once in a while, but that was to be expected. What could I do? My family rarely went to the doctor, and I didn't think having some zits was a disease, so seeking medical care was out. I guessed it was time to rethink the whole dating thing. Maybe there was something wrong with me.

I'd like to say that my failed attempt at getting a first date didn't bother me too much, but the next time I summoned the courage to ask a girl out wasn't until two full years later—in the high school band room, no less.

Cora Peterson was taller than me. When you consider that I weighed 112 pounds as a high school junior, you can understand that just about everybody was taller than I was! She was a nice girl with thick glasses and seemed a bit more my speed than Wanda. The junior-senior prom was coming up, and my friends kept asking me who I was going bring. I decided that Cora was going to be my date for the big dance.

Cora played the French horn, and, despite my small stature, I played the tuba. Luckily, the tuba section (there was only one tuba) was near the French horn section. I spent at least two weeks glancing over at Cora near the end of each morning band session. I kept telling myself that I needed to wait until the time was right before asking her. Truthfully, I was afraid of rejection and I just kept stalling. Finally, it was the Friday before the Saturday dance.

It was now or never! As the other kids stood up and filed out of the band room, I peeked around from my brass hiding spot. There she was, putting her music away. All systems were go, and I slid smoothly onto the chair beside her.

"Hi, Cora. How are things going for you today?"

"Oh, hi, Bert. I'm good, how about you?"

She actually remembered my name! This is going great! I think she really likes me.

"Band practice was really fun this morning, Cora. By the way, do you have a date for the prom?"

"No, I don't."

Great! I thought. *She doesn't have a date, so maybe she will go with me. Now is my chance to finally get a first date!*

"Would you like to go to the prom with me?"

"No, Bert, I can't go with you."

Now, wait a minute. She said she didn't have a date and she didn't say that she wouldn't go with me, so what does she mean she "can't" go with me? This dating is more complicated than I thought! What gives?

"Why not, Cora?"

"It's too late for me to go with you. I don't have a dress, so I can't go. Thanks for asking me, though. Bye!"

Cora stood up and walked away. I was totally relieved and completely happy! She hadn't actually rejected me! She really hadn't said no; I was just too late to get the date. What a victory! This was real progress. *I think I am getting kind of good at this dating thing!*

One year later, I was a senior in high school and I still hadn't had a date yet. I was working at a local hotel as a dishwasher and janitor. The night desk clerk was a young man who was attending the junior college in town. He mentioned to me that his cousin was in my class. Her name was Carmen Miner. He kept teasing me, saying she liked me and she wanted to go out with me.

Maybe, I thought, *the third time is a charm,* so I decided to give it one more try. I saw Carmen in the hallway the next day.

"Hi, Carmen, what's going on?"

"Not much, Bert. I'm heading to algebra."

"Any chance you are free Friday night? I thought I could pick you up and we could go to a movie together." *Hey, I'm getting more relaxed around girls, and talking to them isn't as hard as it used to be!*

"Yes, Bert, I'll go with you. What's the movie you want to take me to?"

Of course I had no idea what was showing that night. There was only one movie house in town, and it showed only one movie at a time, but obviously, I hadn't thought this one out too carefully.

"Don't worry, Carmen; it's a show that I know you are going to like. I'll pick you up in my car at seven o'clock."

I would like to say that we had a great time and this was the start to a beautiful relationship, but that's not true. In fact, after I asked Carmen out, I looked in the paper to see what movie was playing. It was *Patton*! In retrospect, it was not the best choice for our first date. To make matters worse, my car broke down before the date, so I had to borrow my father's giant old Ford station wagon. It wasn't just our first date; it was also our last.

Interacting with the opposite sex has never been easy for me. It was especially difficult when I was inexperienced and shy. Maybe I'm not as smooth as all the other guys, but I sure can be lucky. After all, I married the best girl on the planet despite myself!

Fill 'er Up!

When I was a young man, motor oil ran through my veins! Nearly every thought I had was focused on buying a car. Back then, I could have told you the year, make, and model of any car on the road just by seeing the taillights. When arguing with each other about who made the best cars, my friends and I used phrases like "found on road dead" and "fix or repair daily" to describe Fords. An admonishment like "Get the women, the children, and the Chevys off the streets!" was in reference to a Chevrolet. I would lie awake at night trying to decide what my first car would be. I visualized a two-door, candy-apple red supercharged muscle car with dual exhaust and Hurst floor shifter. And who was responsible for such an exhaust-fume clouded mind? My father, of course!

I was born when the family was living in the back of a gas station in tiny Saint Charles, South Dakota. It's correct to say that the station was at the edge of town, but then, every building was at the edge of town, because there were only twenty people living in the entire place! At the station, Dad sold Standard Oil products and did mechanical work. In those days, no gas station ever sold candy bars or groceries like they do today. You made your money selling gas at twenty-six cents a gallon and getting your elbows greasy with engine work. To keep our family in bread, Dad also sold Pioneer seed to area farmers and raced a stock car on the dirt-track circuit each summer weekend.

Just when things seemed to be working out, the state came along and relocated the highway. That killed the business, and Dad had to close the station. Not deterred, he went to the next town down the road and ran the only gas station there. That town was Herrick, the home of my mother's family. There were a hundred souls there, so Dad had more customers. My memories of that place included a mountain of worn tires out back, holding inner tubes under water to find the leaks, and the smell of burning sulfur patches. Dad taught us boys early on how to check the gap on a spark plug or watch the timing light, but when his father-in-law offered Dad a chance to take over the family farm, we left the station and became farmers just outside of Herrick.

Later on, having a clean, well-maintained car was a point of pride in my family. The garage was full of tools from those gas-station days, and we were allowed to use them as long as we put them back where they belonged. Dad couldn't afford new cars, so we learned how he evaluated the used vehicles he was interested in.

After we lost the Herrick farm, Dad became a telegrapher for the railroad. Around age fifty-six, he lost his railroad job and couldn't find any work. Dad and Mom then sold their house and headed back out to Herrick, where they bought back that same gas station. When I drove from Minneapolis to help them on the weekends, I would pass their first station in St. Charles. The building had collapsed. Out back, I could see Dad's stock car rusting in a field.

When we turned sixteen, our parents let us buy our first cars. My father had only one rule: We had to have twice the money in the bank that the car cost. Since I had saved $800, I went shopping for $400 vehicles. I came home with the best my money could buy: a small used white English Cortina. My dad shook his head in disgust at my purchase of a foreign car. "Won't last," he said. Three months later, I proved him right by racing it on a back road and blowing the engine! When I had built my bank account up again, I went out and purchased my dream car—a 1968 candy-apple-red four-door Dodge Coronet 500 with dual exhausts, black leather seats, and four on the floor. Talk about an excited kid! When I switched on the ignition, the oil in my veins started to boil!

Light the Oven

My mother used to say that I learned by attending the school of hard knocks. I never seemed to do things the easy way, and I often had to learn by making mistakes. On one hand, it's good to learn from one's own mistakes. On the other hand, some mistakes can actually be fatal. I am not sure why, but when I was young, I liked to blow up things. Eventually, this led to a lesson that I would never forget!

It all started when I was playing with matches. My brother Dave and I would wrap a small piece of aluminum foil very tightly over a wooden match head. Then we would hold a lit match under it, and when the foil got hot enough, the match would ignite. The foil funneled the burning sulfur out the back like a rocket engine and the match flew a few feet into the air.

When the Fourth of July came around, we had access to a few of the things we wanted. Do you remember bottle rockets? Put one of those little guys in a pop bottle, light the fuse, and then stand back. The rocket would shoot about fifty feet up and then explode. Well, I didn't need the bottle! I could just hold a rocket in my hand, light the fuse, and then throw the rocket in Dave's direction. He started throwing them back, and then we had a bottle-rocket war going! What could possibly go wrong? I wonder what Mom thought when she pulled our burned shirts out of the laundry basket.

We bought strings of Black Cat firecrackers and boxes of the really big firecrackers called M-80s. Just lighting a string and watching them pop was not good enough for me. I cut them open with a knife and stockpiled enough powder to fill a piece of old pipe. After inserting a fuse, I had a pipe bomb that would blow a sizable crater in the ground. Try that today and you'll likely be arrested! When firecrackers were no longer in season, Dave and

I learned how to make our own gunpowder. We put our friend Sam in the hospital twice during that phase!

Combining model rockets and gunpowder culminated in excitement that I will never forget. There is still an unexplained black spot on the city water tower. One mishap resulted in our friend Doug losing his hearing for a few days. Despite all these antics, I was never hurt and continued to have a cavalier attitude toward explosions. Then I got my first real job.

In the days before motels, most small towns had a large hotel in the downtown district. Such a business would serve as a center of commerce for visitors and local businessmen. I worked at one such establishment called the Gardston Hotel in Estherville, Iowa. It was an old brick structure that was three stories high, making it the tallest building in town. It was one of many hotels that were owned by a crabby old guy. Believe it or not, his name was Mr. Ed Boss. Mr. Boss drove into Estherville once a year. He came in a fancy old Rolls Royce; boy, did that car stand out in town!

My first job at the hotel was as a pot scrubber. You can imagine how exciting that was! I ended up doing lots of different jobs, however, including work as a dishwasher, waiter, bellhop, janitor, and short-order cook. I couldn't cook much beyond breakfast and sandwiches, but I learned a little that I still use today.

While working as a cook one evening, I was told to make a batch of popcorn for the bar. I poured a cup of cooking oil into a large pot and put it on the burner of the old gas stove. Then I became distracted and forgot about it. Finally turning back toward the stove, I saw flames shooting out of the pot! In a panic, I grabbed the handle and pulled the pot off the fire, but I yanked it too hard and the burning oil slopped out of the pot and onto my right hand! What a burn that was! To this day, the resultant scar on my hand turns blue in the cold.

That same stove was the source of another accident. I always had trouble lighting the ovens on those big institutional stoves.

There were no pilot lights, so the procedure I used was to turn the gas on and then strike a match. Never quite sure where to hold the match, I'd just stick my hand in the bottom of that monstrosity and hoped for the best.

One night, the restaurant was especially busy, and I was struggling to keep up with a run of orders, yet a customer saw fit to request that his piece of pie be warmed up! Microwave ovens didn't exist in those days, so I needed to light the oven and stick his pie in there for a few minutes. I turned the gas on and bent down to strike a match. At that instant, a waitress barged through the door, asking me a question about another order. I stood up, answered her question, and then squatted back down in front of the open oven door. Then I struck the match. I don't remember seeing any flame, just pure yellow light, and hearing a roaring sound in my ears. When I stood up, I smelled my hair burning, so I headed for the pot sink! After I dried off, the horrified waitress told me that my eyebrows and the hair on both arms were gone. Fortunately, my face didn't blister much and I didn't get any scars out of that quick ordeal, but I was really lucky to have been wearing eyeglasses.

A few short years later would find me in front of an Army sergeant, with him teaching me how to fire an antitank weapon. He explained that a rocket was going to exit the front while flames were blasting out the back. If the weapon was not handled properly, the operator (me) or nearby soldiers would be killed. Let me tell you, he had my absolute attention! I had acquired a very serious respect for any kind of explosion or flames. After all, I had learned my lesson the hard way while attending the school of hard knocks!

Fishing for Regrets

One July, I was sitting in my small boat, anchored in the Eau Claire River, when I hooked a nice smallmouth bass. After I pulled it in, I laid him down and took out my camera. At the exact instant I shot the photo, that crazy fish popped right into the air! I'd forgotten to take the lure out of his mouth, so one of the treble hooks was in the fish and the other was hanging freely. In the blink of an eye, that free hook pierced my left thumb and dragged my hand down to the bottom of the boat along with that flopping bass! Boy, did that ever hurt! And there I was, alone in mid-river, four hours of paddling from my car, holding a wild fish down with my free right hand—and I'm left-handed! What did I do? I thought of my dad, and here's why.

My father lived through the Dust Bowl. The Moritzes were sharecropping wheat farmers in central Kansas at that time. He occasionally mentioned stories that included tying a rope from the house to the barn to keep from getting lost, or setting the table with the plates upside down so they stayed clean. Dad described clouds of grasshoppers that ate everything, including the paint off their farmhouse, but when my grandmother told me that she had taken my dad's younger brother to the doctor and had been told he was suffering from malnutrition, I understood what my father had lived through. Maybe that's why fishing seemed so important to him. You see, our family fished to put food on the table.

We started by fishing in Iowa for bullheads. Now, if you've never seen one of these creatures, prepare yourself. Black, ugly, slimy, and decorated with three stinging spines along the body, they hardly look like fish! We would go to the shore of some muddy lake and catch twenty or thirty with hooks and worms. Then at home, Dad would pound a nail through their heads to hold them onto a board, and using his pliers, he'd peel off their skins. Mom would bread and drop them into a sizzling frying pan. Picking around the bones and trying to free our minds of that ugly image, we'd eat our fill night after night! It wasn't glamorous, but it's what we did.

Longing to get onto the water, my teen brother Dave and I made Dad an offer: "You buy the boat, we'll buy the engine." That was affordable, so in short order, we were done shore fishing and after better fish! Crappies and bluegills became our dinner of choice for several years. No more bullheads for us! Since we were now into respectable fishing, Dave bought an occasional copy of *Outdoor Life* magazine and we read about game fishing. We dreamt of hooking giant bass and fighting them to the finish. Dad, however, rejected our fishing ideals. He kept on bringing home the pan fish while we boys branched out in search of the big ones. Open-face spinning reels, ultralight rods, fly fishing, and fancy lures! Dave and I went all out to catch game fish, and we did pretty well. It seemed like the more we caught, the less luck Dad had.

I couldn't fish much when I was in college, but when I came home to visit my parents, Dad and I went out in the boat. You should have seen the smile on his face when he brought in a walleye or two! I remember thinking, *When I'm a doctor, I'm going to take Dad to Canada and he's going to catch fish like he has never done before.* That was a promise that I really meant to keep.

I was a young doctor when I had to take Dad to Mayo Clinic. When the examining neurologist told us that he had Alzheimer's disease, one of my first thoughts was that I had failed to keep my personal promise to take Dad fishing in Canada. I knew then that it would never happen, and it's something that I still regret today.

Looking down at the bass that had hooked my thumb I really had two regrets about Dad and myself: first, that he wasn't with me there to enjoy fishing success, and second, that he wasn't there to help me get that darn hook out of my finger! Using my awkward right hand, I managed to find the needle-nose pliers and take that fish off the lure. Into the water he went, probably laughing at me all the way home! Then I snipped the hook down until I had just one piece still buried in my thumb. Finally using the pliers, I pushed the hook point through my skin until I could grasp its tip and tug it out. Talk about pain relief when that came out! I imagined that Dad was smiling with me as I tossed that piece of hook into the water! With antibiotics and a tetanus shot in my future, I paddled on down the Eau Claire River in search of more fish and another memory of Dad.

Colo

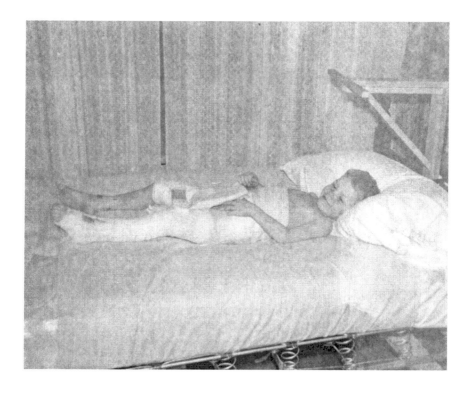

We had to move on after the sale of our South Dakota farm in 1957. My father took the family to a one-room apartment in old town Kansas City, Missouri. My parents and the baby slept in the bed while the rest of us were on the floor in the closet. After a summer course in Morse code, Dad got a union job as a telegrapher with the Rock Island Railroad. His first assignment was to work in the depot of a small Iowa town. Let me tell you about the things I remember from that town—Colo, Iowa.

A population of 564 may not sound like a big city to you, but remember, I was born in a town of twenty people! In Colo, my folks rented an old white wood-frame house with a porch on front and rats in the cellar. We had a crank telephone, and I would lift up the receiver just to listen to conversations on our party line. Mom said we shouldn't do that, but I saw her listening in on the neighbors more than once!

The town seemed to have a lot of crows. They would poop on the laundry Mom hung out back on the clothesline. She had Dad get out his rifle, and he shot those birds right out of the trees in our yard! My older brother, Dave, then collected the dead fowl in a bucket for disposal. In retrospect, the neighbors must have suspected that a family of hillbillies had moved in next door. Mom was still washing us kids in a washtub once a week, so they were probably right!

Having a steady but small paycheck was something new for my father. To help with income, my mother worked out of the home while watching us children. Using a manual typewriter, she typed addresses onto envelopes for a department store. This was well before computers were invented, and Mom could really pound those keys fast. She also supplemented our income by sewing clothes for the family.

I don't remember having many toys in Colo, but I do recall that wanting a toy got me into trouble. Both Dave and I coveted wooden sewing thread spools. Whenever Mom had an empty one, she would yell, "Who wants a spool?" Dave and I would then race each other into her sewing room. We'd stick a thumbtack on one end of a spool. Then we'd hook a rubber band on the tack and thread the rubber band through the middle of the spool. Finally, we would wind the rubber band tight against the other end with a matchstick. When we put the contraption on the floor, it would scoot along like a little car! Dave and I raced these toys and tried to get them to do tricks.

One day, I heard Mom announce a new spool for the taking. The race was on! But I forgot the kitchen floor had been freshly waxed. Scrambling ahead of Dave with victory well in hand, I slid past the sewing room door and then fell hard on the waxy floor! The next thing I knew, I was lying on my back in a hospital bed, looking up at a doctor. I had broken my left pelvis, and he was about to stretch me out for a whole-body cast. I said, "If I don't cry, will you give me something special?"

The doctor responded, "If you cry, you are going to get something you won't ever forget!" The last thing I remember was a nurse putting the anesthesia mask over my face.

I spent two months in Colo lying flat on my back at home in bed. The cast went from my ankles up to my armpits. A wooden stick was anchored in between my knees to keep my legs from moving. I passed the time watching episodes of *Grey Ghost* on our first television set. Dad built an exercise bar over my head so I could work my arms. Eventually, that same doctor cut the cast off with a small saw; talk about itchy, foul skin! At home that night, Mom dunked me right into the washtub!

We left Colo after only a couple of years. This was the beginning of a pattern marked by frequent moves. Dad did well with the railroad, and such moves were the price we paid for our slow march up the economic ladder.

Years later would find me standing in front of an Army doctor for my draft physical. He noticed in my records that I'd had a broken left pelvis. Looking up and down my leg, he commented, "Looks pretty straight. Uncle Sam's going to be happy you had that one fixed!" Now that really hurt!

Now, That's Entertainment!

When I was young, the things that I did to have fun were nothing like what kids do for fun today. We didn't have smart phones, iPods, video games, and the like. We certainly didn't have a few hundred TV channels to choose from! Now, don't think for a minute that I'm about to extol the virtues of the old-fashioned, simple ways of playing as a child. No, my older brother, Dave, and I were intrigued by scientific experimentation, and couch sitting was just not an option. We thrived on learning about the world and taking risks!

Our fun would always start out safely enough. My dad would bring home boxes of used batteries and other scraps from his job. At first we built electric motors and even a radio. We used Mom's wire clothesline for an antenna and listened to shortwave conversations from Australia, but that wasn't enough excitement for us, so we learned to hook fifty or so batteries in series to increase the voltage output. Now we had some real power to play with!

After a school history lesson on the explosion of the *Hindenburg*, we decided that we really needed some hydrogen. Our small Carnegie public library allowed us to read about electrolysis, and before we knew it, we were in the basement with our batteries and a test tube of salt water. We applied a bit of physics, and soon, we had a test tube full of hydrogen and oxygen! Inserting a finger about three-quarters of the way up, we displaced most of the oxygen and kept the hydrogen in the tube. Next we took a fruit jar from the root cellar and righted the test tube under it. Repeating this procedure over and over, we captured a large amount of hydrogen in the jar.

When we figured that we had enough hydrogen, we lit a match and moved it close to the open mouth of the fruit jar. I suppose that it did not occur to us that we were at risk for blowing our hands off, but the ensuing two-foot flame and the sound of the exploding gas was enough to make our hair stand straight up! Suddenly, Mom opened the basement door and yelled, "What are you boys doing down there?"

Dave and I shouted back in perfect unison, "Nothing, Mom!"

Rockets. Good gosh, we grew up when the Mercury, Gemini, and Apollo programs were capturing the imagination of Americans, and we certainly wanted to be a part of that! In those days, you could order almost anything through the mail, so our parents let us order small rocket engines and build our own rockets. (You would have thought that they would have learned not to trust us by now.) Just watching the rockets fly was enough to keep us happy at first. But then things started to get out of hand again.

We put frogs and insects in the nose cone to see how the g-forces would affect them. Then we made a small bazooka and shot at a passing motorcycle! Thank goodness we could not get the missiles to fly straight—the tail sections kept burning off. We tried covering the tails in asbestos (an unsafe choice of materials by today's standards). Next we launched a rocket at the water tower, but we were disappointed to see it bounce harmlessly off, so it was back to the library to learn how flash powder (a form of gunpowder) was made!

One week later, the postman delivered enough phosphorous, magnesium, and Paris green to satisfy a modern-day terrorist! To avoid parental detection, we mixed our first batch of powder up in our friend Sam's basement. He was holding a glass beaker when our concoction spontaneously exploded. He had to go to the doctor to get some glass removed from his forehead. Sam's mother made it clear that we were no longer welcome at their house. Dave was handy in chemistry and eventually got our mixture just right. We launched a series of exploding rockets, and in our imaginations, we started to put some serious fear into our town's inhabitants.

Our rocketing days ended with a bang! I'd built a four-engine missile that we dubbed Big Bertha. As befitted such a masterpiece, Dave fitted Bertha with an extra-large warhead. Knowing that the local police were not going to like it when this thing detonated, we elected to launch it at a remote riverbank site out of town. A good friend named Doug joined us in our bicycle trip to watch the fun.

We started our countdown at ten, and when we got to one, I threw the ignition switch. We'd expected to see that big rocket blast straight up to a thousand feet and then explode into pieces. That did not happen. Three of the engines failed to ignite, and the fourth could lift the rocket only a few feet in the air. To our horror, the rocket hovered there in front of us as the fuse to the warhead burned through! We turned and ran like three scared rabbits. In panicked retreat, Doug slipped and fell on the muddy slope. Big Bertha blew herself to bits a couple of seconds later, and the shock wave darn near knocked us over! Poor Doug complained of lousy hearing for three days!

It's easy for me to complain about today's young people. I think that they are too sedentary and that they don't get enough exercise. I think they should get outside and have some real fun, but when I remember what I did, I'm reminded that too much of my idea of fun can be dangerous to one's health!

Oom-pah! Oom-pah!

Music was his life,
It was not his livelihood.
It made him feel so happy,
It made him feel so good!
        —Harry Chapin

I'm sure we all know that being a teenager and getting through high school are not easy for anyone. Along the turbulent journey, young people discover that they need something they can hold on to, something that becomes a symbol of who they are or who they want to be. Nowadays, it might be a fancy telephone, a big tattoo, or a body piercing. In my day, it was a sports letter jacket, a car, or even a pair of store-bought blue jeans. The choice of symbols available to me was limited, for I wore pants sewn by Mom, I wasn't big enough for athletics, and I had to work part-time jobs after school. Clearly not much to hang my hat on there, so I appropriated the only symbol available to me at the time—the family cornet! Allow me to tell you how well that worked out.

We lived in central Iowa at the time. We soon learned that bands were a hugely important part of Iowa's culture. After all, the then-playing and highly successful musical play *The Music Man* was based on mythical River City, Iowa. Professional bands and school bands were both held in very high regard in Iowa.

Back then, a local television station broadcast a show called *The Bill Riley Talent Hour*. My older brother, Dave, had heard that Mr. Riley was coming to town for auditions. Dave and I were in seventh and sixth grades. We reasoned that a handsome young cornet duo such as ourselves would be a shoe-in for a spot on the program; thus, we needed an instrumental song that would guarantee us a good showing but that was within my early skill level.

We ended up choosing "Oh Christmas Tree!" despite the July audition date.

We might have practiced our number a bit more, but we felt ready when the big day came. Dave and I put on our church clothes, stored our music in our instrument cases, and headed off for the audition. When our turn came up, I began to have some doubts. The lights were hot and bright, and Mr. Riley seemed surprisingly crabby for what I felt was a pair of fine-looking, obviously talented boys—but honestly, our recital did not go smoothly. I got lost in the music and couldn't hit my notes. Fortunately, Dave played reasonably well, so we left with some hope of fame. After watching the talent show every week for several months without getting a stage call, however, we came to realize that we weren't going to be on TV. Ah, failure—a most bitter pill to swallow!

But I wasn't giving up. I kept on going to my music lessons and practicing at home. Upon entering high school, I played in the concert, marching, and pep bands. My parents seemed surprised that I stuck with it. When my younger sister was old enough for an instrument, they gave her the cornet and I received a new Sears trumpet for Christmas.

Man, was that shiny brass horn a beauty! I thought I was really something now, but during my sophomore year, the band director sat me down for a talk one day. He needed a tuba player and maybe I should consider dropping the trumpet. I was stunned! All my talent, and he was canning me? But I looked over to the corner of the band room, and there sat the tuba in all its majesty. It was very big, and light glistened off its bell. I pictured myself in the marching band with an admiring crowd cheering me on. Maybe this tuba thing was worth serious consideration after all!

My switch to the big horn turned out well. Despite my small stature, I had strong lungs and could belt out the notes. As a senior, I entered a contest to find the best tuba player in the state.

I practiced long hours with my piano accompanist. When the big day came, I felt quite ready. Bright lights and nerves were not a problem this time, for I had done this been before. When my turn came, I played the piece perfectly. I was immensely proud— and I was chosen as the second best tuba player in the state!

The first-place player joined the McDonald's All American Band in a trip to Japan. And what honor was bestowed upon the second best player? Unfortunately, it was a winner-take-all contest. Yes, I'd really hoped for first, but I got what every kid needed; I came away with a strong identity, knowing that I had done my very best. I learned how to take a punch and keep fighting. Finally, I had discovered that music was not meant to be my livelihood but that it could still be part of my life.

I ended up switching back to playing trumpet in college. I also played in an amateur jazz band involving much hard work but also immense enjoyment! I did not fulfill my dream of becoming a professional trumpet player, but I acquired something to hold on to during my turbulent teen years, and that's what every youngster truly needs.

Part Two—Life's Lessons

I really haven't learned how to be humble, but the opportunity for study sure has come my way often enough! Like most of us, the times I've appeared a fool or have become embarrassed have generally been self-inflicted. Whether I was driving a bus, getting pulled over by a cop, or trying to be athletic, the result was the same. My uncle Chuck often quipped, "Life is one long lesson in humility."

Raising a child has never been easy; my parents would be the first to attest to that. I really don't know how they managed to survive raising my four siblings and me! If there were any underlying theme to the process, it would have been best described by one word: conflict. Oh, my siblings and I didn't fight about important issues like politics, religion, or morality. Instead, we debated about hair, rock music, and why my older sister spent so much time in the shower!

Growing up was especially hard for me. I lacked confidence and was afraid of the world. You would have been that way, too, if you'd been born in a town of twenty people in the empty outback of America (South Dakota). Like Dylan once sang, "When you got nothing, you got nothing to lose," so I took on challenges to boost my confidence, and in the end, I was the better for it.

Then to confound my life, I became a parent. How many times had I heard the phrase "Pick your battles"? I think that really means "Choose how you want to lose."

The craziest thing about any life lesson is that you can never predict the outcome. Some unexpected twist of fate can change the course of your life forever—case in point: how we each met the love of ourlife. I hope you enjoy reading a few of my life's lessons. You needn't learn from them, but I hope you are reminded of yours.

A Lesson in Humility

Don't we all wish we were a bit more quick-witted—you know, always saying just the right thing at the right time? Years ago, I was standing beside Vice President Hubert Humphrey when he was running for president. A man came up and yelled, "Why are there so many fools in Congress?"

Without drawing a breath, Humphrey shouted back, "Because this is a country of equal representation!" Now, that was a good come back! The only time I nearly equaled that was when a one-eyed patient came into the office. As he seated himself in my examination room chair, he said, "I have only one eye. Can you cut your fee in half?"

"No," I retorted, "the one you have is twice as valuable!" I did, however, reduce my charges accordingly.

Unfortunately, it has not been my habit to quickly say the right thing at the right time. Instead, when I have spoken in haste, the result has usually been disastrous at best! My mother once suggested that I was "popping the clutch to my mouth before putting my brain in gear." I'm better now. Experience has taught me to calm down and think a bit before I speak, but let me tell you about a time when I embarrassed myself by running off at the mouth.

After I had earned a bachelor's degree, I headed off to optometry school in Chicago. It was pretty expensive, and my G.I. bill was running out! I needed money, and I needed a lot of it! I heard that the Chicago Transit Authority (the city bus line) had a program to hire graduate students like me for summer replacement bus drivers. I hired on, got trained, and began driving big buses up and down the crowded streets of the Windy City.

Talk about a small-town kid out of his element! My first summer of driving was pure torture! I was so nervous, I had bus-driving nightmares. I actually started to wonder if I was awake or asleep! Every day, I would report to the central station and get assigned to a street. There were seventeen streets I had to randomly drive. Each street had its own personality and its own problems.

One night I was driving on Lawrence Avenue. This street snaked its way past dilapidated storefronts and run-down row houses. It was known for crazy people who seemed attracted to the bus and the bus drivers. The run ended at Lake Michigan, where I turned the bus around and headed back down Lawrence Avenue again. In an eight-hour shift, I made about ten runs, so there was plenty of opportunity to interact with the locals.

It was a Saturday night, and my bus was jammed with characters of all sorts. One guy smelled so bad, I had to breathe through my mouth. Several passengers got off early and groused at me for letting him on. There was the usual assortment of bag ladies, homeless men, and noisy drunks when someone in the back of the bus pulled the chain. I slid the bus against the curb at the next stop and opened the back door to let them off.

I glanced up at the mirror and saw four or five people shuffling their way toward the exit. After what seemed like an eternity, only one of them managed to get down the steps, and the rest looked like they were bumping into each other. I got impatient. I had a schedule to keep and figured they were all drunk or something. Hardly looking up, I opened my mouth and yelled, "Come on! Get off the bus!" The bus went dead silent, and everybody stared at me. A guy in the seat closest to me leaned over and said, "Hey man, they're blind!" I looked back and saw their white canes.

If a hole had opened up in the earth at that moment, I would have jumped right in! There I was, a student studying to help people with visual disabilities, and I had shot my big mouth off at those who needed understanding most of all! I got right up out of my seat and walked to the back of the bus. After helping them off,

I returned to driving. I'm sure my face stayed beet red, and I was sweating as I drove to the end of the line.

Years later when I was golfing with my uncle Chuck, he hit an especially bad shot and said, "Life is one long lesson in humility." Nobody knows that more than I do! We all have to learn to think before we speak. When we do, we all get along a lot better.

Little Anna

After dating Susie for three months, I knew she was the girl for me! I began to think about asking for her hand in marriage, so I decided I'd better develop a better relationship with my future in-laws. This wasn't going to be easy, because I hadn't made a good first impression on her parents.

I was almost four years older than Susie, and I often wore my old Army clothes when I came to pick her up. Her father viewed me with a measure of suspicion. Then, when I had been invited to eat dinner with the family for the first time, I had just returned from the dentist. My face had still been numb, and I'd had no idea that peas were rolling out of my mouth onto the floor! I wondered why everyone was staring at me during the meal.

To top that off, I had then been issued an invitation to the family Easter celebration. Susie informed me that a special family friend affectionately called Little Anna would be there. Apparently, this elderly woman had the role of family matchmaker, so having her approval would go a long way toward helping me gain Susie's hand! As Easter got closer, the pressure mounted! Before we get into that, however, let me tell you about that elderly woman who would decide if I'd be allowed to marry my sweetheart.

Her name was Anna Metzen, and she had immigrated to the United States from Lithuania. She spoke Polish, Russian, and broken English. She had married but had had no children. When her husband had died, she had taken a cleaning job in the Minneapolis Health Club restaurant. It's easy to remember what she looked like. Less than five feet tall, Little Anna sported curly white hair, and her face was a mass of wrinkles when she smiled. When we visited her small upstairs apartment, she would usually be puffing on a cigarette while talking with her friend named Polish Anna. During our visits, they'd both admonish me to eat more garlic for better health!

As the years passed, Susie and I would make stops in Minneapolis just to visit Little Anna. It was common for her to cook some vartines and insist that I sit at the table as she piled them on my plate! She would also buy us a couple of long, pungent Polish sausages from the nearby meat market. Anna was poor, and we felt bad that she would spend her Social Security money on us; thus, I began to hide a twenty-dollar bill in her apartment whenever we visited. She caught on to this trick, however, and began to follow me wherever I went. I quickly learned that the bathroom was the only place I could hide the money for her!

To celebrate one wedding anniversary, Susie and I decided to take our first trip to Hawaii. Before going to the airport in Minneapolis, we stopped in to greet Little Anna. We agreed not to tell her that we were going to Hawaii. After all, she would have scolded us for "wasting good money" and being foolish Americans.

As expected, Little Anna produced the usual aromatic Polish sausages, and I carried them out to the car at our departure. I remember putting them into the trunk and thinking, *What could go wrong? We'll be back in ten days, and the sausage will stay frozen in the mid-January temperatures.* You can imagine how disconcerting it was when I picked up a newspaper in Hawaii and noticed an article about an unusually strong and long "January thaw" in the upper Midwest! Upon our return, we had no trouble finding our car in the parking ramp—we could smell it! Boy, that was a long ride home.

So, back to that Easter Sunday and my first encounter with Little Anna. I was nervous and unsure of what to expect. In preparation, I donned my only sport coat and tie and proceeded to the crowded gathering. Everyone was eating the really strong-smelling Polish sausage that was a family tradition. Susie escorted me over and then introduced me to Little Anna. Naturally, the whole family had to crowd around us as she looked me over. It was very hard for me to understand what she was saying, but she was cute and most delightful! I noticed that she was squeezing my arm pretty hard. Finally, she reached up and patted me on the cheek. "You are a good boy," she said. Then she turned to Susie and said, "He's a good boy. You can keep him." I breathed a sigh of relief, for I had I had passed the big test!

A Little More off the Top?

I don't know about you, but I find some of the recent trends exhibited by younger people to be a bit disconcerting. Specifically, all that body piercing and those tattoos seem just a little too far out for me. Perhaps this means that I am growing old, but I just can't bring myself to accept those things. Maybe every generation settles on a symbolic way of expressing independence—you know, something that would really bug their parents! For my generation, it was our hair.

Being a family of limited means, we did not have the extra money for visits to the beauty parlor or barbershop. Mom was in charge of family hair care, for she claimed to be a hairdresser. I say *claimed* because we knew that she had at one time attended beauty school but suspected that she'd never actually graduated.

Weekly hairstyling was *de rigueur* at our house. For my two sisters, this meant spit curls with bobby pins, big curlers, and then some hot time under a gigantic hair dryer. When the occasion called for a special hairdo, Mom would glove up and pour on the chemicals for a real perm. Boy, did the house ever stink after that was over!

All in all, though, my sisters had it easy. The real hair conflicts occurred with my two brothers and me because Mom didn't know much about haircuts for boys and men. In the early years, her approach to the male scalp worked well enough to satisfy her. She would take out the electric clippers and buzz us right down to the skin! When she was done, the four guys in our household (including Dad) all looked like jarheads from Charlie Company of the Second Marine Division!

Then one fateful eve, while I was watching a program broadcast in black and white with my father and brothers, the program's host, Ed Sullivan, introduced a new rock band called the Beatles! At the end of their performance, I turned to Dad and excitedly exclaimed, "I'm going to grow my hair just like that!"

He spat out three words that I will never forget: "No, you're not!" Talk about a declaration of war! The generation gap suddenly became a chasm, and the only way across for me was with longer hair.

Month after month, the battle raged as Mom trimmed my hair down to stubble. Finally, after much protesting, she changed her technique. She got out the bowl! At first, this appeased me, until I noticed that I resembled Moe from the Three Stooges and George, Paul, John, or Ringo hardly at all.

My big break for an improved haircut seemed to come when I started my first paper route. Now I finally had money in my pocket and could head straight to the barbershop, so off I went to our town's only barbershop for my first haircut by a professional. I sat down and watched a few men get their hair cut ahead of me. When my turn came, I hopped into the chair and told the barber I wanted my hair left long in the back. Much to my chagrin, he took out his clippers and began shaving it all off! I was stunned and not sure what to do, as I was only eleven years old. When he finished the job, I looked in the mirror and asked, "Why did you do that?"

He replied, "Because your father called and told me to."

I then boldly stood up and said, "Then you get him to pay for it!" With that, I walked out. The following month, I returned and got my hair cut just the way I wanted—and the barber got paid, too!

Some years later, my parents met me at the airport in Sioux Falls, South Dakota. It was on the day of my discharge from the US Army, so I came down the Jetway in my dress uniform. I hugged Mom, shook Dad's hand, and casually pulled off my cap. Dad suddenly glanced at me, and I looked back at him. There I was, with my hair all shaven off again. And Dad? His hair was covering his ears and touching his shirt collar; he even had a moustache! You know, the guy actually looked a bit like a rock star!

How I Met Your Mother

Most of us can perhaps look back and see how an obvious event or some particular influence shaped the course of our lives, yet sometimes even a single seemingly insignificant decision we make can result in profound consequences for our futures. One of the most important decisions any of us can make is in deciding who will be the love of our life. A seemingly insignificant decision on my part would go on to play a most consequential role in how I would meet my future bride. Let me tell you how that happened.

After my stint in the Army, I enrolled in a two-year junior college in Rochester, Minnesota. In due time, I finished my coursework and was about to graduate with an associate degree, but I really wanted to become an optometrist, so I needed to find another college and work toward a bachelor's degree in science. I really had no idea where to go next.

One day while walking down a hallway, I noticed a flyer posted on a bulletin board. It promised a scholarship of one hundred dollars to any student who had at least a B average and transferred to St. Cloud State University. I remember thinking, *No one else is offering me one hundred dollars, so I guess I will go there.* Such a simple decision filled with consequences unknown to me at the time!

A bit of a challenge awaited me while registering for classes at St. Cloud State! You see, I needed an anatomy and physiology class; however, the course was completely full and I couldn't get in. Desperate, I met with the professor and pleaded my case: "I need this class now or I will have to go to college an extra year before applying to optometry school."

"Sorry I can't help you. The class is full," he said.

"I was drafted, spent two years in the Army, and I don't want to get behind another year."

"The class is still full."

He seemed unmoved, so it was time to play my last hand. "If you let me in, I promise you I will be the best student in the class. I'll sit up front, ask good questions, and get an A on every test. You won't regret it!"

What a sight I must have been as he looked me over. I stood there wearing my Army-green field jacket, combat boots, and black Army "birth control" eyeglasses. He took pity on me and said, "OK, but I want to hear from you each day!"

A deal is a deal, so each time the class met, I did exactly what I had promised. Unknown to me at the time, there was a cute, Irish-looking girl named Susie Quigley sitting in the back of the classroom. It was pretty easy for her to notice me—after all, my hand was up in the air almost nonstop!

I was highly motivated to get good grades in every class I took. I spent hours in the university library working hard. In fact,

I spent so much time there that the librarians felt sorry for me! One day, a librarian asked if I would like a private room for quiet study. She said those rooms were usually reserved for graduate students and she felt I would make good use of one. I happily accepted and moved right in.

On December 31, while preparing for the national optometry examination, I noticed a note taped to my study room door. It was a holiday card from Susie! I called her up and asked her out on our first date. We spent the next evening skating on Lake George. My ankles hurt so much that I had to kneel in a snow bank. She threw snowballs at me, and we laughed together. Three years later, I proposed to her on New Year's Eve. That was thirty-seven years ago. And that's how I met your mother!

Man Overboard!

Susan and I had been out of college for about three years when we made a move to Eau Claire. With that move, we decided that we really had to buckle down and pay off our hefty student loans. We lived through some lean times, paid off the loans, and then redirected our efforts toward a down payment on our first house. Let me tell you, I felt pretty special the day we walked into that new home!

Later that week, we took a drive around Lake Wissota. It was a sunny summer day, and we gazed over the blue water. There, in the middle of the lake, was a beautiful tall-masted sailboat. Feeling financially powerful (only partly correct, as I now had a home loan), I turned to Susan and said, "Let's buy a sailboat. I've always wanted to learn to sail!" This seemed innocent enough. After all, how hard could sailing a boat be? Little did I know that I was about to embark on an adventure that would put life and limb on the line!

After a bit of searching, I managed to find a small used sailboat to my liking. It was of a wet-board design, which meant that it was a simple, flat-hulled vessel with one sail. I'd heard that the wet-board design was best for learning, so it seemed like a good choice; however, the boat we bought was called a Laser. The name should have been a warning to me, for I later discovered it was actually a racing boat designed with experienced sailors in mind!

With a Lake Wissota Yacht Club membership in hand, we headed out to the lake for our first attempt at sailing. I'd read the first chapter of a book Susan had given me on sailing and thus was certain that I could sail. There were lots of members at the club that day, and they watched as we proudly pushed our little sailboat away from the sandy shoreline. At that moment, a light breeze filled the sail and, much to my chagrin, we immediately rolled sideways! Not knowing what to do, we were both unceremoniously dumped into the cold water! And how far out did we sail? Well, not very far, because the tip of our short mast actually touched the shoreline!

It was a rough start, but giving up was not an option for me, so a couple of years later, I not only had mastered sailing but was able to compete in the yacht club's races. Happily, my efforts with the little Laser brought me a second-place trophy in a big regatta at season's end.

Encouraged by that accomplishment, I though it was time to look for another boat. This time, I intentionally bought a bigger racing boat called a J Scow. With a sixteen-foot hull and a twenty-four-foot mast, she was a thing of immense beauty as well as speed.

It was late in the season, but I couldn't resist taking her out on a maiden voyage before the winter set in. Susan was working, so off I went by myself to Lake Wissota one morning late in October. It was cold and windy, but I raised the sail anyway and headed out to the center of the lake. I had quite a blast playing around, with the boat healed way over and flying over the waves.

Just in my moment of glory, the wind conducted a wicked shift! Over the boat went, dumping me into the surprisingly cold water a short distance from the boat! Worse yet, the mast and sail fully sank below the waves. This is called going turtle, an unfortunate condition in which the boat is completely upside down, with the mast pointing at the bottom of the lake. Now I was in real trouble! I collected my wits, swam to the boat, and clung to the upturned hull. Eventually, I hoisted myself out of the water and held on the best that I could. In the several minutes that had passed, the wind had risen, with large waves now washing over the hull and threatening to push me overboard! On top of that, I began a hard shiver due to the cold!

With the combination of cold, strengthening waves, and

wind, I was rapidly becoming exhausted. I looked around and knew that I couldn't swim for shore. What's more, there wasn't another boat on the entire lake—and for good reason! It obviously was not a bright idea to be out there under these conditions.

I held on for what must have been another hour. To my good fortune, I finally spied a speedboat mercifully heading my way! Two youngsters had seen me and were coming out to tow me ashore! Later as I lay shivering on the sand, I knew that I would always be grateful to those young people. I also promised myself never to take that kind of risk again!

A few years later, Susie and I were vacationing in Bermuda with friends. We had arranged to stay at an old seaside hotel that supplied a sailboat with each room. My friend Paul and I decided to take a boat into Hamilton Harbor. It started out as a very pleasant sail with low waves and a light breeze. I was at the tiller, and I said to Paul, "Let's go just a bit farther out." (Remember the promise that I had made to myself about not taking any more risks?) As we rounded a point of land that defined the end of the harbor, the waves suddenly surged in behind our boat and the wind immediately picked up!

I could hear panic in Paul's voice as he said, "We're out of the harbor and in the open ocean! We had better turn back!" The waves were now four-foot rolling swells, and they were quickly spiriting us away from land. I tried to turn us windward but lost control. Then the sail whipped around, so we both had to duck to protect our heads from the crashing boom. Finally as the boom snapped taut, we could hear the sickening sound of sailcloth ripping!

Suddenly, we found ourselves dead in the water with our sail flapping uselessly and our boat heading out to sea. "Paul, where do you think we are going to land?" I asked.

"England," was his curt reply! Fortunately, Paul had brought along a plastic jacket to use as a windbreaker. Utilizing some quick thinking and ingenuity, we tied one sleeve to the end of the sail. In holding on to the other sleeve for dear life, Paul brought our useless sail back into action. With that, I was able to swing the bow around and beat a hasty retreat to shore. Old terra firma had never felt so good before!

I had started sailing when we bought our first house. Another life-changing event, the birth of our daughter, ended my sailing career, but my sailing adventures will always be with me; likewise, I hope, will the good fortune that helped me survive them!

Move to the Back of the Bus, Please!

Being an optometrist is the greatest job in the world! I treat eye disease and correct the vision of patients of all ages. I get to share in their lives as they move in and out of my office every few years. But as good as my occupation is, it's not the most exciting job I have ever had. Let me tell you what it was like to be a city bus driver in Chicago.

The Chicago Transit Authority hired graduate students as summer replacements for vacationing union drivers. I have to admit that as a small-town kid from South Dakota, I was more than a little concerned about the traffic and the crowded polyglot neighborhoods, but the authority paid almost thirteen dollars an hour, and in 1976, I needed the money to help pay for optometry school. I took a chance and signed up!

Bus driver training was short and to the point: They taught us how to open and close the doors, how to pull into traffic, and how to read a schedule. I began to get suspicious that I was in over my head when they demonstrated an emergency radio alarm system that was hidden on each bus. This allowed the bus driver to secretly summon a Chicago policeman when needed. When we were given a lecture to discourage us from carrying knives, pistols, and brass knuckles, my attention began to shift from how to open the door to who might be coming through that door!

After driving a fifteen-ton bus up and down the street a few times, we were ready for our final lesson. A huge empty parking lot was sprayed with water and motor oil to simulate Chicago streets right after a rain. We took the bus up to speed and then, at the command of our instructor, stomped the air brake to the floor and spun the steering wheel. That bus did two complete circles as I hung on for all I was worth! It was a life-altering experience, and to this day, I apply my brakes gingerly right after it rains!

My first day on the job was absolutely terrifying! I put on my uniform and reported to the Jefferson Park Bus Terminal. I walked up to the dispatcher, and he handed me a manual that had the maps and schedules of seventeen routes that I would drive, a different one every day. My first assignment was Milwaukee Avenue. The schedule indicated that I would have to drive down to the Chicago Loop and back eight times that day. The dispatcher asked me if I spoke either Spanish or Polish. He didn't seem impressed when I answered in the negative. I found my bus in the barn, hidden among 200 others. I had to ask the kid who was sweeping out the busses how to drive out of the yard and which direction to turn so I could find Milwaukee Avenue.

Pulling up to my first stop more than a half hour late, I was greeted by fifty hot, crabby Chicagoans saying things I was glad I couldn't understand. I tried to get them onto the bus as quickly as possible. Preparing to pull into traffic for the first time, I looked to my left, checking my mirrors, and snapped the doors closed. I put my foot on the gas and cranked on the steering wheel, and the bus lurched forward. At that moment, I heard a woman's scream! I looked to the right, and there, pinched between the bus doors, was a waving arm! Outside the doors was an old woman running alongside the bus, shouting in Polish! I stopped the bus and let her in. She stormed up the steps pointing to her arm and yelling at me. I have no idea what that woman said, but I do recall letting her take a seat without having to pay the forty-five-cent fare.

During my second day on the job, I found out why each bus was equipped with the emergency police-call system. I was headed south on Central Avenue with a full load of people at eleven thirty at night. Two guys got on at Harrison Street, and as I pulled the bus forward, one of them took out a pistol! He stood right beside me with the gun pointing toward the back of the bus as his buddy relieved my riders of whatever they had. Thinking that it was the right thing to do, I inched my left hand toward the "hidden" emergency switch on the dash. The character with the pistol saw what I was doing. Looking down at me, he said, "Don't worry, we're not going to hurt you. Our neighborhood needs this bus service." Though I wasn't reassured by his concern for his community, I did understand that I had just lost the firepower battle. I kept driving while they finished robbing the passengers. They got off a few blocks later.

This was how my part-time career as a Chicago bus driver began. I stayed on that job for four consecutive summers. There weren't many dull days! A long list of memorable experiences would have to include having my bus set on fire twice, being robbed by a guy with a sword, letting a load of riders off in wet cement (their footprints can still be seen along Lawrence Avenue), and getting into a wrestling match with a street person named Milwaukee Mary.

This job actually had more benefits than just combat pay. This small-town kid learned that *inner city* wasn't a bad phrase. Those hardworking blue-collar people had a feeling of family and community that can come only from a shared circumstance. For all the people I was afraid of, there were many more who helped me and respected me for the job I did.

Having the greatest job in the world hasn't made me forget how I got there. My work for the Chicago Transit Authority gave me memories that will never be forgotten.

Easy Rider

When Dad was hired as a telegrapher for the Rock Island Railroad, one of his union benefits was a week of paid vacation. In the early years when money was scarce, a vacation for our seven-member family meant only one thing—a trip to see the relatives. A hot summer drive to either South Dakota or Kansas in the crowded family station wagon without air conditioning was quite an ordeal! And we never stopped at a restaurant or bought cold pop at a gas station. For road refreshments, Mom would pack bologna-and-margarine sandwiches in plastic bread bags, and she'd serve warm drinking water from a couple of fruit jars.

A few years later, with the family growing up and funding not so tight, we switched to a new vacation style. Dad would rent a pop-up camper and he'd tow it behind the station wagon. We kids would still argue over the rear-facing back seat of the station wagon, and we still ate Mom's sandwiches, but we traveled west to see the beautiful country we lived in! The best trip we ever made was to Yellowstone National Park. Dad and I caught a bunch of cutthroat trout, and Mom fried them over a fire. I will never forget that. That was not my favorite vacation, however; my best vacation was when I once traveled alone.

I was discharged from the Army in June of 1973 with plans to attend college in September. I had some time to kill so decided to head back to the folks' house in Iowa. It was great to see them, but I had this crazy feeling I was out of place and had to get out on the road, so on a whim, I bought a used motorcycle and decided to head west. My brother Dave was soon to be discharged from the Air Force in Montana in August, and I set my sights on meeting up with him.

Now, don't jump to any conclusions about my trip. I did not buy black leather gear or a big Harley-Davidson motorcycle or join a gang! I spent all of $300 buying an old Honda 350, a motorbike that most would consider way too small for a long road trip. I put one change of old Army fatigues into a backpack along with an old canvas tarp and a jar of Vaseline for waterproofing. With $400 in my pocket and an Army field jacket on my back, I kick-started that baby and waved good-bye! I might not have looked bad to the bone, but in my mind, I was king of the road!

Let me tell you, riding well over a thousand miles on a Honda 350 was nothing short of brutal! The vibration and the wind were always buffeting me. A gust of wind once blew me into a ditch in South Dakota, with my leg ending up against the hot exhaust pipe. Bugs were a constant menace at highway speeds. Though I had a helmet visor that helped with the critters, on occasion, a large one would smack into my chin!

Riding toward Bozeman, Montana, late one day, a cold front came through, producing a dandy thunderstorm. I stopped to put on a light rain suit, but the wind tore it off and I got completely soaked. Usually, I slept along the road in a ditch, using the canvas tarp and the bike to make a lean-to shelter, but that night, I was so cold that I decided to spend some money and stay in a campground. When I got to my campsite, I was shivering so hard, I couldn't start a fire or change out of my wet clothes. A couple of hippies in a nearby Volkswagen minivan noticed my plight and invited me over to their fire. The bowl of hot soup they gave me felt like a lifesaver!

My tour of the west brought me to Shoshone National Forest in Wyoming. I pulled into a free campsite and set up right next to a fast-moving mountain river. Soon, a pair of guys riding big motorcycles and wearing black leather pulled up next to me. As they unpacked their gear, I couldn't help hearing that they were mad at each other. Apparently, their tent was contaminated with oily Vaseline! You see, in those days, a biker mixed old engine oil with some Vaseline and used it to lubricate the drive chain. They must have done a poor packing job, for their oil bottle had broken. I watched them struggle to get their tent up.

With nightfall coming on, one of the guys decided to get firewood, and to my utter amazement, he headed straight for the water! He must have had his eye on some driftwood on the other side of the river, as he plunged right into white-water rapids! Getting out no more than a few feet from shore, he was knocked over by the heavy current and began to yell for help. His partner and I ran down and hauled him out. Looking like a half-frozen trout, he sheepishly thanked us.

Well, that pair of guys turned out to be two brothers from New York City—that explained why they were such lousy campers! The next day, we agreed to ride together, although they were concerned that my little Honda wouldn't allow me to keep up with them. After a couple of days, they headed west, and I turned north into Yellowstone Park. One morning, I awoke in my lean-to with a moose head poking in at my feet! Another day, I was stopped on the road and a grizzly bear walked so close that he almost hit my front tire! I sure could have used doors and windows just then.

Finally, it was time to meet my brother in Great Falls. I got up very early on my last day in Yellowstone. My New York buddies had suggested that my bike would not make it over the high-altitude continental divide, so I wanted an early start before the traffic picked up. Sure enough, partway up that mountainous road, my Honda started sputtering, and then it died! The engine couldn't get enough air, so I had to get off and push it uphill. Getting over the top of the divide felt great, especially when the engine purred back to life for that final downhill run into Montana!

I sold my motorcycle for one hundred dollars to an Air Force captain at the Great Falls Air Base. Dave and I jumped into his '69 Mustang and drove straight back to Iowa. I finally took off my field jacket, and felt much better. I was home and ready to get back into civilian life. That Honda 350 was my first and last motorcycle. I can't imagine another vacation as good as that one!

No Common Sense

Susan and I have the secret to a successful marriage. We are perfectly matched for each other. She is hardworking, nurturing, and a good decision maker, while I'm detail-oriented, logical, and scientific in my approach to life's problems—but I have one tragic flaw: I've absolutely no common sense! None at all. Period.

Thank goodness my wife makes up for me in this category. If you are a patient of mine, you might be surprised to learn this. I certainly appear to be of sound mind and reasonable judgment, but appearances can deceive! After all, I put my friend Sam in the hospital twice, caused good buddy Doug to go deaf for three days, and convinced my brother to drive a car into a deep pool of mud. Allow me to give you a few more examples of situations in which I would have been well served by even a smidgen of common sense.

Our daughter, Anna, learned the hard way about my lack of common sense. When she was first learning to walk, I decided to make a video of her ambling about the house, so with the camera glued to my face, I followed her along, giving words of encouragement: "Keep going, sweetie, keep walking. You are doing great!" However, I failed to notice that she was too near the doorway to the basement stairs. "Just a little more, honey." Imagine my horror when she suddenly disappeared from view, tumbling downward and bumping off each step! (The video recorded all the action, ending with her wailing at the bottom of the stairway.) Susan came rushing around the corner just in time to see me sheepishly standing at the top of the stairs, camera in hand. "No common sense" were the next (but not the only) words that I heard!

When Anna was seven years old, she became active in gymnastics. As a good father, I wanted to encourage her, so I built a balance beam for her practice in the basement. Thinking that I'd covered all the bases for a safe design, I built the beam only a few inches above the floor. The next day, while reading the newspaper in the kitchen, I was pleased to hear her already practicing on the new beam. Suddenly, she began to scream, claiming that she had hurt herself! I figured she was overreacting, so I called out, "Just come upstairs and let me see." I walked over to the stairwell just as she neared the top. Glancing down the stairs, I noticed blood on every other step! I quickly scooped her up, and then the blood really came pouring from the bottom of her foot! Susan, an experienced emergency room nurse, rounded the corner and immediately said, "For Pete's sake, hold that girl upside down!" The bleeding stopped immediately. After the wound was stitched and normalcy returned, I figured that I'd better take a look at the beam. Of course, I had forgotten to round off the corners of the lumber, and a sharp edge was the problem. I should have known!

I almost set our first house on fire —twice! Hoping to save a few bucks, I'd cut firewood and burned it in the basement fireplace. One morning, I dutifully scooped the hearth clean of what I thought were cold ashes and then dumped them into the garbage can. About an hour later, we smelled smoke. Rushing into the garage, I peered through the thick cloud and saw flames erupting from the can. I managed to haul it out and heave it into a snowbank. The garbage can was made of plastic, no less! No common sense.

My second attempt at involuntary arson was at the burning season's end. After emptying the cardboard box that had stored the wood, I decided to cut up the box and burn it in the fireplace. I then put a match to the cardboard, and it took off nicely. Little did I know that creosote might have accumulated in the chimney and that a cardboard fire might burn hotter than my usual wood fire. What happened next was nothing short of terrifying! A rather peculiar, soft rumbling noise in the flue quickly grew to a loud roar! Not sure what to do, I rushed outside in the dark and was mortified to see what appeared to be a fire-spewing volcano in place of the chimney! After the fire department had left, my wife just shook her head. I knew what she was thinking—no common sense!

By now, you've probably surmised that I pose a danger to others. Rest assured that my tragic flaw has found a way of including even me in its consequences. Knowing this, Susan wisely puts my chainsaw in her car's trunk on her way to work whenever I have a day off!

In understanding my own flaw, I chose fishing as a hobby. After all, how could I get into trouble doing that? Accordingly, Susan gave me a small, lightweight fishing kayak. For additional safety, she presented me with an inflatable life vest. Fitted with a water-activation mechanism, the vest is designed to inflate automatically using compressed gas. Despite the mechanism, I found the vest to be lightweight and comfortable.

On my first trip out with the new gear, I began by moving slowly down the Eau Claire River, casting for bass and having a great time. Then I snagged what must have been a submerged stump. From my boat, I could see my lure stuck near the bottom in waist-deep water. Not willing to break the line and lose a three-dollar fishing lure, I hopped out and waded over. Even after a bit of finagling, that darned lure refused to budge, so I took a breath and bent into the water, expecting an easy retrieval. My ears were barely beneath the water when I heard what sounded like a shotgun discharging close to my stomach. Instantly, I bobbed up like a cork in a barrel! It's hard to explain how foolish I felt with that inflated vest around my neck and that lure still on the bottom! Later, I learned it would cost me thirty dollars to recharge the vest. A poor investment for a three-dollar lure, perhaps? No common sense!

One midsummer day the following year, I was out fishing the Eau Claire River again. It had been a good day with lots of smaller bites. Finally, I hooked a big smallmouth bass. Quickly dropping the anchor, I played the fish over to the boat, but just as I started to scoop it into my net, that lunker gave a flip and I dropped both net and fish into the water! Holding the rod in my other hand, I turned and saw the net floating downstream. At that moment, the bass jumped and jerked the rod clean out of my hand! I watched in utter amazement as the rod slithered upstream in the opposite direction of the net. What was I to do? Undaunted, I hopped out of the boat and waded after the rod. After a few minutes of searching frantically, I was relieved to spy the rod's cork handle on the river bottom. Not wanting to lose my favorite rod, I knew my only choice was to dive for it. Remember my inflatable life vest? Well, it wasn't on my mind at the moment, and sure enough, it did its inflating trick right on cue! The big fish was still on the hook, but it sure didn't look like a thirty-dollar piece of meat!

Dirty Harry once said, "A man's got to know his limitations." Well, I know mine (most of the time, that is). I've managed to survive my lack of common sense by marrying a woman who possesses more than her share of it—and thank goodness for that!

No Common Sense, Part Two

It's hard to put into words how disappointed I am in my fundamental lack of common sense. I often wonder how I ended up so afflicted. As a youngster, I was inclined to test the limits around me, and to that end, I caused my folks more than enough grief. Maybe in the checks and balances of nature, my lack of common sense was payback for those unorthodox behaviors early on. When I was two years old and we were living on the farm, our dog was chasing a rooster. Running for its life, that darn bird scooted right between my legs! The dog followed, and I was upended in the barnyard! My head landed on a piece of glass. My brother Dave contends that inadvertently tight stitches are to blame for my behavior problems. Who knows? But somewhere along the line, this slightly devious boy was transformed to an absentminded and slightly dangerous man!

I have always liked fire and explosions. That's not good when a lack of common sense is your tragic flaw. The trouble started when my teen brother Dave and I placed an order with a chemical company for pure sodium. We were surprised to see that the postman delivered it to us in a sealed metal can. Inside, we found a creamy yellow substance the consistency of putty; it was packed in thick oil to keep it from exploding on contact with moisture.

Dave and I excitedly biked out to the nearest creek, precious sodium in hand. With the flick of a pocketknife blade, we dropped a morsel of it into the water. The little chunk floated, spun around, smoked a bit, and then self-destructed with an anemic crackle—nice, but not the action we were hoping for, so we decided to try a bigger piece ... a much bigger piece. We stuck a golf-ball-sized hunk of the element onto a rock and then flipped it into the water. Wow! Seeing that explosive column of flames and water shoot skyward was an epiphany for me! If only I had known then what trouble my commonsense deficit and fire would cause me in the future!

My wife, Susie, and I live in the country. We have forested property through which the Eau Claire River runs. Ten years ago just after we moved in, I noticed numerous piles of brush scattered around the house left by the previous owners. It concerned me that this dry wood would serve as fuel in the event of a forest fire, so I gathered the wood and placed it in a safe open space for burning. It turned out that the ideal spot was the center of our backyard tennis court.

Days of lugging brush away from the house and out of the tick-infested forest edge finally paid off with a giant pile ready to burn. My history with fire had not been good, so wisely, I had a shovel and water hose at the ready. A little gasoline, a match, a windless day, and ten hours later, the bothersome brush had been reduced to a mound of smoldering embers. A job well done!

A week later while working around the property, I glanced toward the tennis court and saw the ashes. I carried a large metal (yes!) garbage can to the court, shoveled it full of ashes, and then dumped it out in the woods. It was around five in the afternoon. Hot and tired, Susie and I decided to take a break on the deck and relax. Opening a beer, I told her what I had been doing.

"Are you sure the ashes weren't still hot when you dumped them out?"

"Of course I'm sure, honey. They have been there all week and there is no way they can even be a bit warm after all that time."

"Well, did you actually stick your finger in and check?"

Now, at this point, I knew I hadn't really checked properly, but I didn't want to look bad in front of my wife, so I did what had gotten me into trouble as a child. I lied.

"Yes, honey, I actually put my hand into those ashes, and they were a cool as a cucumber!"

I had just about finished off that bottle of beer when the wind shifted and I smelled something. "The neighbors must be burning again today," I reported to Susie. "I smell smoke." A few minutes later, the wind came up again and some smoke drifted over our deck. My neighbor was a good quarter of a mile away, and it struck me as odd that smoke was drifting all the way from there.

"I hope that crazy neighbor hasn't put the darned forest on fire!" I quipped. We both stood up and looked through the trees just past the tennis court. Not only did we see more smoke, but we also saw flames galloping in the woods!

"Fire!" Susie yelled. "You put our woods on fire!"

On the verge of total panic, I furiously laced up my boots and charged into the woods. Susie was right; a charred circle about half the size of our house was ringed in flames and spreading in all directions. Flames even began crawling up tree trunks. Because I am a guy, my first thought was avoiding the embarrassment of calling the local fire department! I realized that time was short and quick action was vital.

Susan began rolling the hose out and filling buckets of water. I grabbed a spade and worked the fire line as fast as I could. Two hours later, covered in soot and sweat, we were exhausted but the fire was out. My wife just looked at me and shook her head. "You have no common sense. What were you thinking?"

Staring beyond her at the tennis court, I could see where the "cold" ashes had burned a hole right through the blacktop surface. I knew exactly what she was going to say when I had to explain that one too!

Talking Too Fast

One Sunday morning a few years ago, my wife; our daughter, Anna; and I decided to drive up to the Ice Age Trail near Bloomer for a hike in the woods. We do this each fall just as the leaves are turning. Heading out of town, I engaged the car's cruise control a tad early. As luck would have it, I got a speeding ticket. Sitting in the car, waiting for the county deputy to hand me a citation, I looked over at Anna and suddenly was struck by a feeling of déjà vu. Here's why...

The last time I had gotten a speeding ticket, it was 1971. Now, don't think for an instant that I have not been guilty of occasionally speeding during the previous forty-one years! On the contrary, I am just as guilty as most drivers and have been pulled over a number of times; however, I've usually been able to talk my way out of a ticket. Let me tell you about one of those times!

For the past twenty-five years, I have helped run the main telescope at Hobbs Observatory in the Beaver Creek Reserve. Every Saturday night, young Anna would accompany me to the observatory. Together, we'd show members of the public various objects in the night sky. Our routine would be to arrive at nine p.m. and work until all the people had left. Then we would stay an extra hour or two so we could look at some interesting galaxies or nebulae on our own.

One night when Anna was about eleven, we completed our work and started the drive home at about one a.m. It was an enchantingly clear night, and the sky was full of bright stars. As we drove toward Eau Claire, we became thoroughly engaged in discussing the evening's celestial sights. Suddenly, my rearview mirror lit up with the glare of red and blue flashing lights! I glanced down at my speedometer and was stunned to see that I was driving seventy miles per hour in a fifty-five-mile-per-hour zone!

I felt quite embarrassed to have my young daughter with me as I was caught breaking the law. Dutifully, I pulled over to the side of the road and waited. Out of the squad car marched a tall highway patrolman with a big Smokey the Bear hat on his head. As I rolled down the window, he made a point of leaning in close to me and saying, "Sir, you were speeding. Why are you out here this time of night?" It seemed obvious he was suspicious I'd been drinking, so my brain kicked into high gear to marshal some kind of defense.

Now, whenever I go into that mental mode, the mouth is sure to follow! I sucked in a lungful of air and really let fly! "Sir," I stammered, "I am here with my daughter. We were at the observatory, using the telescope, and now we are going home. I was telling her about Saturn, which is just over there to the south, and I did not know I was going too fast. In fact, sir, this car is very powerful and smooth, so it is hard to tell the speed. I haven't had a speeding ticket since before I was in the Army. I didn't mean to speed. It's just that—"

Suddenly, Anna interrupted me, nearly shouting, "Dad, stop! You are babbling!" The patrolman burst out laughing as he took my license and headed back to his squad car.

As we sat there in silence, I wondered how much the ticket was going to cost me. I apologized to Anna for embarrassing her. When the patrolman returned, he handed me my license and a white slip. "Sir, I'm going to give you a warning ticket. From now on, drive the speed limit. And yes, you were babbling!"

My uncle Chuck often says that life is one long lesson in humility. Getting a speeding ticket is proof of that. Sometimes it's just better to keep quiet and take your medicine, so that's what I decided to do recently as I mailed in a check to the Chippewa County Clerk of Court!

Three Strikes and You're Out!

Aren't kids wonderful? Every parent surely can recall an incident or two in which their child's actions in public caused extreme embarrassment. Still, we love our children, so we continue to expose them to as wide a range of life's experiences as possible. In principle, this sounds admirable, but this attitude can buy us some trouble. Allow me to explain.

Do you remember Art Linkletter's TV segment "Kids Say the Darndest Things"? Well, my daughter, Anna, learned one day in kindergarten class that smoking was unhealthy, so the next time we were in a restaurant, she stood up in our booth and loudly chastised a nearby woman for smoking by announcing, "You're being bad—stop smoking!"

My wife and I enjoy art, and we like visiting art museums in any city that we happen to be in. We saw no reason to change that habit after Anna was born, so we decided that she would accompany us on future visits. It was easy at first, because she didn't walk. Ah, but then came the toddler years and beyond!

A long weekend trip to Chicago had us walking up the steps of the world-class Art Institute of Chicago. What a fabulous place to visit! At the entrance, I reminded myself to keep little Anna close by, given the sensitive nature of the exhibits.

The first room we entered was full of works by the famous Impressionist painter Claude Monet. There was a guard in that room, keeping a watchful eye on the truly priceless paintings. I really did try to hold on to Anna, but I became so involved in the paintings that she slipped away from me. With an outstretched arm, she immediately charged toward a million-dollar painting! I saw what was happening, so I lunged forward, catching her just in the nick of time—but not soon enough to escape the attention of the guard! We were escorted out and found we ourselves standing, red-faced, on Michigan Avenue.

Six years later, while visiting relatives in San Diego, we spent a day in Balboa Park and the world-famous San Diego Zoo. What a great place for our ten-year-old daughter to have experienced! Then we headed over to the San Diego Museum of Art. By that time, Anna had developed some appreciation of art. She even had a favorite artist—Georgia O'Keefe. We moved through the museum effortlessly, and Anna was being very good—that is, until we rounded a corner. There, on a low, special display stand, stood a large O'Keefe painting. Recognizing it instantly, Anna walked right up to it and reached out to touch it! As the guard was escorting us out, I turned to him and said, "We've been thrown out of better places than this. We were tossed out of the Art Institute of Chicago."

"You're right," he responded, "that was a better place than this. Have a nice day, sir."

A couple of years later, we began planning for a trip to London. Luckily, a London-born patient of mine came in for an examination. I asked her for museum suggestions. "You must visit the Wallace House in Westminster," she said. "The art is excellent and the great hall is full of medieval antiques." We took her advice and placed it on our agenda for an afternoon visit.

We found Wallace House to be delightful and everything she had promised, with room after room of pleasant art; what's more, there were no other visitors or guards! When we entered the great hall, I could see that the four walls were covered with antique swords, shields, and all manner of ancient artifacts, but the main attraction was placed directly in the center of the hall. It was a replica medieval knight in full armor and mounted on a huge black stallion.

We split up and wandered about the perimeter of the great hall. Suddenly, the quiet of the moment was shattered by the blaring of an emergency siren! I glanced back at my daughter, who was standing near the knight and stallion. I walked up to her and demanded, "Did you touch that horse?"

"No, Dad, I did not."

A guard burst through the doorway. He walked right up to my daughter and said, "I was watching you on the security camera. I saw you touch that horse!" And the rest is history, which I will leave for you to determine…

Our daughter continued her enjoyment of art with some pleasant results. Some of her sketches and paintings now adorn the walls of one of my examination rooms. I'm very proud of them, but sometimes when I look at them, I am reminded that kids say (and do!) the darnedest things!

Part Three—Families

As the old saying goes, you can pick your friends, but you can't pick your relatives. Both sides of my family started as poor German farmers, but that's where the similarities end. Once on American soil, most went off in so many different directions that I've lost track of most of them. Occupations of the relatives I have known included paratrooper, judge, crop duster, race-car driver, priest, and bootlegger. It's a wonder that only one of our clan did time!

I have my share of boring relatives, too. This includes the usual assortment of nurses, accountants, engineers, and the like. Most of my relatives have been respectable, but that's not to say they were all likable. When you read this section, you will learn how many of them lived and how a few of them died.

Several of these stories will describe relatives who were inspirational, who were our leaders and set examples I hoped to live up to. A few stories include relatives who set the wrong kind of example, which every family has some of.

I think it is common for each of us to look at our relatives and believe there can be no others like them on the planet. You are about to learn that this is simply not so. The diversity, the failures, and the successes of my people are a mirror of those of your family. Within that pack of zany relatives is your genetic inheritance, your culture, and your values—and just think, you didn't get to choose any of them!

Honesty—Not Always the Best Policy?

In most ways, my parents were much like many parents of their generation: hardworking, not well educated, thrifty, and with strong values. I would guess that this describes your parents too; however, we all remember certain traits that set our parents apart from all others. Let me tell you a bit about my mother and about a special trait that she had.

My mother was named Genevieve Pearl Moritz (nee Rust). She was never more than five feet tall, so she had to sit on a thick book when driving a car. She ranked second in her high school graduating class of three students! After graduation, she worked as a hairdresser, a farm wife, and finally as a hotel desk clerk. My mom got a real dose of liberation when she was issued her first driver's license. To remind my father of her newfound freedom, she began to smoke a pipe! The trait that set my mother apart, however, was her tendency toward impulsive honesty while talking with others. There were times when she could be brutally honest to a fault. Boy, did that cause her trouble! Perhaps some examples are in order.

While the seven of us were sitting down to family supper one eve, my mother noticed that one of my sisters had developed a slight bulge in her tummy. Looking her in the eye, Mom asked, "Are you knocked up?" Now, that kind of talk was never allowed in our house, much less used by Mom in front of Dad, but her impulsive need for honesty just got to her, and she couldn't help blurting it out!

Another time, Mom spoke out in front of family and visitors on the day of her and Dad's twentieth wedding anniversary. After a celebratory supper, we were all sitting in the living room, reflecting on their marriage. Then my oldest sister Bobbie asked, "Mom, if you had it to do all over again, what would you have done differently?"

Without hesitation and without thinking, Mom replied, "I would have married a richer man, and I would not have had Paul!" I can still remember the odd look on my youngest sibling's face when he unexpectedly learned that he was unwanted!

A few of Mom's frankly honest proclamations were issued to me. Years ago, I drove my new girlfriend home from college to meet the parents. Susie had red hair, a light complexion, and a face full of freckles from her Irish descent. When I introduced her, the very first thing Mom said was "You don't feel bad about those freckles, do you?" To this day, Susie reminds me of that event!

Finally, let me tell you about a most memorable experience. At nineteen years of age on a hot summer day, I was waxing Dad's car in the driveway. The postman came up to me, handed me a letter, and then walked away without saying a word. I opened the letter, read it, and then went into the house. When I saw my mom, I said to her, "Mom, I've been drafted."

She took one look at me and said, "Well, at least you'll be a small target." To this day,, I can remember feeling the hair on my head standing straight up!

From a distance provided by time, we can see that everyone's parents did many of the same things to raise us and to help us get started in our lives. It was the differences in our parents that kept our lives interesting, though, and that's what we now remember the most.

Planes, Trains, and Automobiles

I miss my father. I think about him every day. Norbert Moritz was a humble man, and in many ways, he was quite common. The oldest son of poor Kansas sharecroppers, he left school after the eighth grade to take over the family farm. He married a farm girl, and together, they had five children. The longest trip of his life was driving a Ford station wagon to Yellowstone Park with the kids stuffed into the back.

Not having much education, Norbert struggled to earn enough money to keep his young family going. We lived in the back of a gas station when I was born, we lost a farm in South Dakota, and, at one point, the whole family lived in a tiny apartment in Kansas City, where the three oldest kids slept on the floor in a closet.

Somehow, this humble man managed to raise five children who ended up with a combined total of twenty-nine years of college education—and now those kids of his are spread out across this great nation, working in medicine, engineering, and industrial development. How did that happen? I'll tell you how it happened. It was with planes, trains, and automobiles!

What Dad lacked in education, he more than made up in other ways. He was a hardworking, risk-taking, competitive daredevil! Let's start with the planes. As a boy, Norbert went to air shows that were complete with biplanes and wing walkers. Oh, how he yearned to fly, but with his father dying, he was permanently grounded in the wheat fields of Kansas. That is, until World War II came along. The country needed pilots, and it needed them right now. Afraid that he was too short to qualify, Dad did pull-ups with weights on his legs on the day of his physical. He just made it! Norbert joined up, and he was trained to fly, first as a civilian and then in the Army Air Corps. The airplanes that he flew included a Ford Trimotor, a DC-3, gliders, and numerous small craft. After the war, Dad bought a tail dragger from the Army and retrofitted it as a crop duster, but this scheme to make a buck failed when the plane crashed into a field.

Dad didn't have enough money to maintain his own airplane, so he volunteered as a pilot for the Civil Air Patrol. Years later, when I was driving Dad to the nursing home, we had just sold everything he owned. Looking out the car window, he spied a small airplane in the bright blue sky. Alzheimer's disease had yet to steal his memories of flying, and he turned to me and said sadly, "I sure wish I could have just a couple more hours up there."

Now let's talk about trains. Trains played a stabilizing role in my father's life. After taking three weeks of class to learn Morse code, Dad got a job as a telegrapher on the Rock Island Railroad. With a steady paycheck, things were looking up for the family. He traded his old car and his labor for a down payment on our first house. A good worker and a quick learner, Dad became a depot agent and finally an appointive agent. We moved to ten towns before I finished high school.

Dad's big break came when he was given a promotion to trainmaster, but when he was asked to show his college diploma, the promotion was taken away. That experience motivated my dad to go back to school. At age fifty-two, he earned his GED. That was a proud day in his life!

The Rock Island Railroad went bankrupt in 1980. Thus, at age fifty-six, my father was unemployed. He interviewed for jobs on other railroads but never got them. "Age discrimination is behind it," he once told me. Norbert might have been down, but he was not out ... which brings us to automobiles.

Remember how I mentioned that we lived in a gas station when I was born? Norbert grew up fixing engines on the farm. After marrying a South Dakota girl, he took a risk and bought a small Standard Oil gas station in St. Charles, South Dakota. With only twenty people in that town, he needed business from the nearby highway, and he had three extra jobs to help with income. They were delivering fuel oil to area farms, racing a stock car on dirt tracks, and even running a bit of moonshine to dry counties!

The end to his first gas station came when the state government moved the highway away from the station. Dad's second gas station came right after he lost his railroad job in 1980. He sold his house and bought a station in Herrick, South Dakota. This was a town of seventy people, and this station was on the same highway as the first one. Norbert put a trailer house out back and fixed up the station. I helped him paint it. Hoping to attract business, he added dry goods and a meat case. When farmers stopped in, there was always free coffee on the burner and cards on the table. Dad built up the business, and after a couple of years, it was a success. Then Dad developed Alzheimer's disease. He was sixty-two years old, and the final stage in his life had begun.

Planes, trains, and automobiles were more than just my father's livelihood. They were vehicles that helped my family navigate the roads of our lives. We are who we are because our father did what he had to do.

A Tale of Two Families

Some time ago, I was reading a newspaper published up north called the *Barron News Shield*. Two articles, both published in the same edition, struck me. One was titled "Deaths from Cancer in Barron County Down." On the next page was another titled "Deaths from Heart Disease in Barron County Up." I suppose that this should come as no surprise. After all, we all have to die from something, but it's one thing to die from disease or natural causes, and quite another to die from something preventable. Let me tell you about the frank differences in the cause of death for each side of my family.

My father lived with his parents and his seven siblings on a small farm in Kansas. They were sharecroppers and thus were not immune to hard work. Growing up a Moritz meant working the wheat fields and heading for the root cellar during storms.

My mother lived with her parents and her four brothers and sisters on a small farm in South Dakota. My mother's high school graduation class had three members, and if you were called a sod buster, you still had grass sprouting on the top of your house. Growing up a Rust meant making sausage, pounding the cabbage into kraut, and hoping for rain.

Now, there were two main differences between the Moritz side and the Rust side of my family: bad genes for the former, and a bad habit for the latter.

Henry Moritz, my grandfather, carried a gene for a disease called Huntington's chorea. This is a neurologic disease causing a slow, steady degeneration of the brain. Symptoms often start when the affected person is in his or her early thirties, and it is first noticed when the person has uncontrolled movements of the limbs (the word *chorea* is Latin and means "to dance"). Huntington's disease, as it is now called, is fatal, and patients often live the remainders of their lives in nursing facilities, dying in their forties or early fifties. Grandpa Henry died at age fifty-two.

Each of my grandfather's children had a 50 percent chance of inheriting the gene and having the disease. Five of his eight children also died from Huntington's disease. Luckily, my father did not inherit it. I remember growing up with no Moritz grandfather and with Moritz aunts and uncles who were symptomatic with Huntington's and died young.

Now, my mother's side, the Rust family, had good genes, but everyone in the family smoked cigarettes like they were going out of style! I can remember my grandparents smoking while we kids sat around the kitchen table playing hands of Russian rummy. My mother and her siblings were always smoking, too. And how did this bad habit affect the health of my Rust relatives? Grandpa Rust developed pancreatic cancer, and he died at home. The last time I saw him, he was very sick and he said to me, "Whatever you do, kid, don't smoke!" I never forgot that. Then Grandma Rust died from emphysema. Uncle Larry died from a stroke at age fifty-four, Aunt Pat died from lung cancer, Aunt Joann died from breast cancer, and my mother died from emphysema. And what about the last surviving Rust aunt? Aunt Ann is still alive and well at age eighty-eight. You see, she was the only one who stopped smoking many years ago while still healthy!

There are certain aspects of our lives that we have no control over; the genes that we've inherited from our parents are a good example. Then there are aspects of our lives that we *can* control. Choosing to smoke or not to smoke cigarettes is one of those. With the certainty of death in each of our futures, we should strive to do the best we can with the cards that we have been dealt!

Against the Odds

A few years back, my mother's side of the family gathered for what would pass as a family reunion in South Dakota. We were all invited to the Centennial "Squeal Meal" in Herrick. Actually, any human who had ever been associated with this town of one hundred souls was invited! My brother-in-law from Idaho nearly won the longest-beard contest. That, along with the pulled pork sandwich, was the highlight of the event.

Looking around at the crowd, it was obvious there were lots of farmers in attendance. Strong people, really—deeply tanned everywhere that showed, except their foreheads. Hard work gave them taut arms, knees going bad, and weathered faces but with a calm demeanor that revealed an acceptance of their reliance on fate. I know of no other people who can work so hard for an entire year, do everything right, and then, at the last minute, lose it all to an unpredicted quirk of the weather. And do those folks give up? Do they roll over and quit? No. They shrug their shoulders, accepting that things were "spotty" and that their farms happened to be in the wrong spot. They then start over the following spring, year after year.

It's bad enough that farming is a hard way to make a living, but it's dangerous too. I remember visiting with a neighbor who had a tractor roll over on him. His wife found him pinned to the ground with the hot exhaust pipe in his thigh. He showed me a scar so deep I could have put my fist into it. In the old days, missing fingers were the norm. Just add fickle weather to these injuries, and you have enough to challenge even Prometheus. More than one farm wife has looked long and hard at her husband, wondering if he was going to break this time around.

Owing to a shortage of hotels or motels near Herrick, our family boarded at a game ranch twenty miles from town for the "reunion." As I drove up to the place, I could see that the fields were full of pheasants! The house that we had rented was a large hunting lodge. The owner said that he released thousands of pheasants each year and hunters flew in from as far as New York City to hunt the birds.Early one morning, I looked out the window and saw two pheasants sitting on the hood of my car! Game ranching is a creative use of such poor farmland; too bad we hadn't thought of this years ago when we farmed in South Dakota.

The hunting lodge sat on a slight rise. On land as flat as central South Dakota, this meant we had a view that stretched for miles in every direction. The sky was enormous, and the plains felt endless. The rain had been generous for once that year, and the fields of corn and milo stood tall. On the last afternoon of our stay, the temperature was nearing one hundred degrees and the humidity was high. We weren't aware, but the local folks knew what'd be coming next.

As daylight began to fade that evening, I stood on the veranda with my brothers and sisters, facing west. Where the land met the sky, a thin line of low clouds stretched across the entire horizon. As we watched the clouds advance toward us, a hot breeze suddenly arose on our backs. Then it became a steady wind. I remember thinking, *Winds from east not fit for man or beast.* The entire front of clouds bore down on us, sucking our air toward it. Growing in power by feeding on heat and humidity, the clouds piled upward. The coming storm towered tens of thousands of feet high, dark with water, and about to crush us. The east wind died, and suddenly, the wind barreled in from the west with a blast of cold air on our faces. The assault had begun!

It was dark. The wind whipped our clothes so hard, I could hear them flapping. I leaned into the rising wind with lightning overhead and claps of thunder following. We stood there feeling so alive! The first drops were scattered and huge, splatting on the lodge walls or stinging our skin. Then the hail came, drumming on the roof and forcing us indoors.

The ochre light of the just-setting sun signaled that the advancing line had moved beyond us. We emerged to a glistening, wet, surreal landscape deep in color and hope. Watching the receding storm race over the prairie to the east, I wondered whose fields had just received this needed rain. Whose fields were now flattened and doomed to failure? Maybe the odds are always stacked against some men and their families, I don't know. But what I do know is that not many quit.

Aunt Joann

When we lived on the farm in South Dakota, we didn't have a television. Entertainment for us was getting all the kids together in Dad's Ford station wagon and heading off to a steam engine show. Boy, did my father love seeing those giant antique traction engines shaking the earth as they drove slowly past, throwing cinders and belching smoke! There has always been a dark side to farm machinery, though. Serious injury, even death, was common among farmers on the prairie. At those steam shows, I noticed that some of the older farmers who demonstrated the machines would be missing fingers or even limbs.

As we have all learned, life is not equally fair to everyone. On my mother's side of the family, there was one person who was given a particularly raw deal, yet she became a role model for the rest of us. It all started by having some innocent fun on the family tractor.

My grandparents, Frank and Audrey Rust, had five children who lived beyond infancy. The youngest of their four daughters was Joann. At five years old, she was a cute redheaded happy girl who played with her siblings around the farm. The kids liked to walk beside the steel-wheeled tractor as their father drove out to the fields. Then when he wasn't looking, one of them would hop onto the outside of one of the mammoth wheels and hold tightly to the thick metal spokes. As the tractor rolled forward, they would be turned upside down, slowly going around and around. One day, little Joann gave it a try, but she became frightened and let go in panic. Frank heard the other kids crying out, and he found Joann lying behind the tractor. She was dazed and had a bump on her head, but otherwise, she seemed fine.

About a week later, Audrey began to recognize that their daughter wasn't acting right. Joann didn't seem to be paying attention to anyone. A visit to the local doctor revealed that she was completely deaf in both ears! A specialist confirmed that both auditory nerves had been damaged and that Joann would be deaf for the rest of her life. Frank and Audrey then sent their youngest daughter to live at the South Dakota School for the Deaf in Winner.

Joann grew to be an amazing adult! Talk about a classy woman! She had a good job in the newly formed computer division of Honeywell Corporation. Never married, she wore nice clothes, was well read, and traveled all over the world. In her later years, she loved boating with friends on nearby Minneapolis lakes.

Joann had a boyfriend who was a popular singer in England. She would watch us as we listened to his records, and she wanted us to describe what his voice sounded like. When she came to visit us, she would drive down from Minneapolis in a black and yellow 1966 Ford Mustang. What a sharp car! My dad always took it for a drive to check for problems, and then we would change the oil.

So how did Aunt Joann succeed despite her disability? Back in South Dakota at the school for the deaf, they had taught her how to read lips. Signing was not taught at that time. Joann became very good at understanding the speech of others, for she was a terrific lip reader! I remember when she was interviewed on a television show about the deaf. The host did not believe that she could read lips well, so he told her a joke. Aunt Joann laughed so hard that they had to go to a commercial break! In short, that woman retained quite the sense of humor. She embraced life, and she enjoyed it!

But just like the dark side to farm machinery, there is a dark side to being deaf. Joann was an easy mark for thugs, and she was occasionally robbed both in and out of her home. And sometimes, she did not understand important issues. When diagnosed with breast cancer, she must have become confused about her treatment options. Unfortunately, by the time my mother found out about Aunt Joann's cancer, it had progressed and the treatment failed.

Aunt Joann was fifty-four years old when she died. During the funeral service, a beautiful bouquet of white roses was placed near her casket and an English fellow stood at the back of the church.

Joann is buried out on the South Dakota prairie beside her parents. Reflecting her sense of humor, her epitaph reads: "I'd Rather Be Boating!" She was an exceptional person, and a visit to her grave is always inspirational.

Black Sheep of the Family

We have all heard the phrase "You can choose your friends, but you can't choose your relatives." My mother's side of the family was a mix of tough and hardworking German and Scots–Irish folk. They came into this world with nothing, and they left it with about the same! Along the way, a few of them got into some trouble. Let me tell you about one of the black sheep in our family.

When I was born, my family lived in the back of a gas station located in St. Charles, South Dakota. There were about twenty people in that town, and my mother was embarrassed that it was so small. She listed the nearby town of Herrick on my birth certificate because it had a population of over one hundred!

The leading residents of Herrick were my grandparents, Frank and Audrey Rust. I say *leading residents* because they owned the liquor store—and what a place this was! The liquor store was a converted wild west saloon complete with a long wooden bar and a potbellied stove. The heavy smell of chewing tobacco and spilled whiskey filled the air. One of the highlights of my youth was to go into that place and listen to the old men tell stories as they were warming themselves around the stove. Here is the story that they told about my great grandfather.

Years ago, William "Bill" Eiler farmed in the hilly breaks near the Missouri River. Besides farming, he had a knack for judging horses, so he made extra money as a horse trader. He was also known to be the best square dance caller around. In addition to these talents, he had a special knack for drinking harder than most.

In those days, procuring a good drink was almost impossible, for these were the Prohibition years. To cope with the problem, Bill built himself a large still in the early 1920s. He kept it in the barn. The still's output was greater than his own impressive needs, so he sold the extra whiskey to the nearby Lakota (Native

Americans). These sales added an extra measure of risk to what was already an illegal activity, for selling liquor to the Indians was a federal offense, but ol' Bill was a risk taker, so he kept a sharp eye out for the lawmen.

Everything had been going just fine until one spring morning in 1928. Bill heard a sharp knock at the farmhouse door. When he answered it, his neighbor said, "Better get that still dumped; the feds are coming right behind me!"

Bill turned to his fourteen-year-old daughter, Audrey (my grandmother), and told her to run out to the barn as fast as she could. "Dump the still over before they get here. I gotta hide the liquor bottles!"

Sure enough, two federal agents came to the door and demanded to search the entire farm. They marched Bill all around, and when they came to the barn, they could see Audrey staring over the adjacent fence at the pigs. When Bill looked in, he could see that every hog was dead! He was sure mad about losing those animals, so he then turned to Audrey and gave her heck for dumping the half-made moonshine into the pigpen!

Bill Eiler was arrested, tried, and convicted of bootlegging. My great-grandfather was then sent to Fort Leavenworth Federal Penitentiary in Kansas, where he served a year behind bars!

We have all done things in our lives that might have kept our relatives from being proud of us, but in each family, there is usually one person who has distinguished himself or herself by getting into more trouble than all the rest. That's why they are called the black sheep of the family, and Bill Eiler was ours!

A Man about Town

Richard "Dick" Quigley was my father-in-law. He died at age eighty-four, and I was asked to give the eulogy at his funeral. I was happy to do it. After all, Dick was a great guy and we'd had years of fun together.

I thought of Dick as a man about town. He had his own one-man real estate and insurance company. Dick knew absolutely every human being who resided in his hometown of St. Cloud, Minnesota, and in every midwestern town that Dick and I visited together, it never failed: there was always someone Dick knew! Along with all those friends and business acquaintances came many good stories. I want to tell you a few stories about Dick, and then I will tell you what I said at his funeral.

When Susie and I got married, we didn't expect my future in-laws to spend a lot of money on our wedding. When I told Dick that we would probably elope, his seemed surprisingly happy. In fact, he promised me if we did elope, he would give us $2,000. So, Susie and I were married in Chicago. We had only two wedding guests, who also served as witnesses. Susie's wedding dress cost twenty-two dollars, and I made the wedding cake from a box that said "Betty Crocker" on it. Finally, our liquor bill was just under three dollars (the cost of one bottle of Cold Duck wine).

Shortly after the ceremony, Susie informed her parents that we were married. They immediately sent gifts, including kitchen items, wine glasses, and a check for $500. On our first visit to St. Cloud, I casually mentioned the promised money. Dick just smiled and suggested patience. For the next twenty years, the balance of that $2,000 became a running joke between us. I would ask for the money, and he would remind me that it was building interest! I'm still waiting.

I began practicing optometry in Eau Claire, Wisconsin, in 1982. Shortly afterward, Dick came to Eau Claire for a visit. We took him out to dinner at a local supper club. As we were being seated, an elderly woman waved to me. She was with her husband and a large group of people. I didn't recognize her, but I dutifully waved back. At the end of our meal as we stood up to leave, Dick leaned over to me and said, "If you're going to be successful in this town, you have to learn how to build a business. That woman obviously is a patient of yours. You need to go over there and say hello to her and her family."

I knew Dick was right, so I walked over to the table, smiled at the woman, and said, "Hello, it's so nice to see you this evening." She seemed genuinely delighted as she got up and clasped my hand. Turning to the other tables crowded with people, she loudly announced, "Everyone, here is someone that I want you to meet. This is the doctor that I have told you all about. He has helped me so much." And then she turned toward me and said, "You are the best eye doctor I have ever known. Thank you so much, Dr. Redmann!"

Well, since my last name isn't Redmann, I summoned the best smile I could and thanked her. As I was putting on my coat to leave, Dick asked, "How did it go?"

I responded, "She said I was the best eye doctor that she had ever known." Dick nodded approvingly.

The next day, Susie had a job interview at a local hospital. Dick and I didn't have much to do, so we came along and waited in the hospital lobby. Bored, we simply chatted a bit and observed the people coming through the front door. Unknown to us, a Weight Watchers class was about to start, and one obese person after another walked in. I saw Dick raise his eyebrows over and over again. Then he turned to me and said, "Do you think that you've chosen the right profession?"

Surprised, I asked, "What do you mean?"

"Well," he responded, "you might do better in this town with a fast food restaurant!"

Because his wife, Helen, had passed away from cancer, Dick lived alone in their country house. Susie and I would occasionally drive up for a visit. One time, Dick was in the middle of trying to buy a new car. He had answered a newspaper ad and had arranged for the seller to drive the car out to his home for inspection.

A young man emerged from the prospective vehicle, a nice Pontiac sedan that seemed to be right for my father-in-law. After a test drive, Dick began negotiating. At one point, he looked the young man in the eye and asked, "Is this car going to last very long?"

Seeing Dick's gray hair, the young man quipped, "Sir, this is the last car that you will ever have to buy!" Selling life insurance must have prepared Dick for that one-liner for he took no offense and bought the car. By the way, he lived long enough to buy one more vehicle!

Dick's been gone for many years now, but I continue to recall that man about town and his stories. Because stories were such an integral part of his life, I included one in his eulogy. Here is what I said at the funeral:

> Richard Joseph Quigley was born on January 18, 1918, to well-situated, well-educated parents. Dick always spoke of a happy childhood. He would reminisce about watching the blacksmith, horseback riding, and wandering the streets of downtown St. Cloud. When I think about Dick's life, I can't help but think about how intertwined his life was with his hometown. He attended Holy Angels Elementary School and Technical High School. He went to college for two years.
>
> When World War II started, Dick joined the National Guard. In 1942, he was trained to be both a glider pilot and a cryptographer. Dick served in England with the 466th Bombard-

ment Group. He was a sergeant during the offenses of Normandy, northern France, and the Rhineland. Dick loved to recount his adventures and travels in the military. Some of us have even heard those stories more than once!

When the war ended, Dick returned to St. Cloud. He met and married Helen Barres in 1949. After a year in Chicago as a baby food salesman, they returned to St. Cloud to raise a family. They had eight children, including two sets of twins!

An unforgettable and humorous event occurred during a radio interview when Dick was out buying bananas one day. Noticing that he had bought a lot of bananas, the radio announcer asked Dick how many children he had. Dick answered, "Three!" Unknown to Dick, the entire family was at home listening to the radio. To this day, the siblings are still wondering which three he was admitting to!

Helen died in 1981, leaving him a single parent and without a mate. This was a difficult time for him. Dick eventually moved into a downtown apartment, and his life got better. He lived independently and happily for many years. When Dick moved into assisted living, his children were there for him. Dick was a son, a brother, a husband, a father, a father-in-law, a grandfather, and a good friend. Each of us, friend or family, has a great memory of Dick that will last a lifetime.

Contrasting Memories

The human mind is hard to understand. Take memories as an example. Isn't it odd how some event or experience from the distant past can suddenly resurface in our minds, completely fresh, as if it just happened? Such a memory can often be activated by a particular sound, a facial characteristic on a stranger, or even the smell of a food. I want to tell you about triggered memories that I have for each of my parents. I wish I could say that both memories are pleasant, but...

Each time I smell cigarette smoke, I experience a memory of my mother, Genevieve. She had smoked Camel cigarettes for as long as I could remember. Through the years, she made valiant efforts to quit, but she never made any headway. At around the age of fifty-five, she began to develop breathing problems and was given a diagnosis of emphysema. Even then, Mom continued to smoke; it became apparent that she was heavily addicted to cigarettes.

As my mother's health failed, my father, Norbert, was diagnosed with Alzheimer's disease. They both ended up in a nursing home located in Boise, Idaho. Mom was on oxygen, but she was getting weaker. After two trips to the Boise hospital, Mom knew that she did not have long to live, so she told us that she would never go back to the hospital again. She was unable to walk, so she sat in a wheelchair, breathing from a tank of oxygen.

I flew out to see Mom and Dad that Christmas. Mom had just turned sixty-two. After a few good days' visit, it was time for me to return to Wisconsin, so I first said good-bye to Dad. We left him sitting in their room as I wheeled Mom down to the exit door with me. Saying good-bye to her was incredibly hard. Here was this tiny, frail lady—my mother—struggling to breath enough to say good-bye, and we both knew that this would be the last time we would see each other. As I fumbled out the door, I turned around for one last look. She was crying. It is this image that returns to me each time I smell cigarette smoke.

Dad worked for the Rock Island Railroad for more than twenty hard years. The company went bankrupt, and he then became unemployed. After a year of not finding work, he sold the house and he and Mom moved back to South Dakota. Dad then bought an old gas station, spruced up the outside of the building, used big red letters to name it Herrick Station, and put in a repair shop. Next, he painted the interior and brought in groceries and a case for frozen meats. Finally, he put in a card table and a big coffeepot. He was open for business, and boy, was he proud of that place! To his first customers, Dad gave monogrammed key chains and pens.

I was working at a clinic in Minneapolis at the time when I drove out to see the new business. As I came up the road, I could see that the old place was looking pretty spiffy! I pulled in next to a gas pump and went in. Seated at the card table were four farmers playing rummy and laughing it up. The smell of freshly brewed coffee was in the air. I looked over and saw Dad behind the new counter. He had one foot propped up on a stool, and he was wearing his new Standard Oil cap. When he looked over at me, he smiled from ear to ear! As we shook hands, Dad said, "Need some gas, Bert?"

"You bet I do, Dad!" I responded. We walked out and filled the tank together. Now, the tri-tone of a forlorn train whistle triggers that delightful image of Dad broadly smiling in that old South Dakota gas station. It sure makes me feel good to remember that moment!

It's not likely that all our memories are happy. Some are poignant while others fill us with warmth, but memories form an important part of each of us. As I've tried to show here, I don't think that any of us would ever give that part away.

Grandma Moritz

Over the years, I've enjoyed hiking in the woods with a good friend. On one excursion, we happened upon a part of the forest that had been badly damaged by a recent windstorm. Looking at the destruction, my friend turned to me and said, "People are like trees—some bend in the storm and others break." Let me tell you about my grandmother, because she is a great example of someone who did not break despite all of the stormy events in her life.

Anna Marie Hake was born in a small farmhouse in 1897 on the Kansas prairie. Her parents were sharecroppers who never owned any land, and that was to be her fate as well. She married Henry Moritz, and they had eight children. At first glance, her life seemed difficult, but not more so than that of others in her community. When it came time for fieldwork, she led the horse and Henry pushed the plow. Young Anna could sew, churn butter, cook, butcher the animals, do the laundry, and raise children. She loved to make quilts, and she had a strong religious faith.

As you know, times were tough for everyone in those days. Despite the Great Depression, clouds of grasshoppers, and the Dust Bowl, the growing family held together. When the youngest boy became sickly, Anna took him to the doctor. One can only imagine how she felt when the physician diagnosed it as malnutrition, and that the treatment was to give the child more to eat.

Three of her older sons served during World War II, and two more sons served in the Korean Conflict. You might think that this life was enough to put anyone to the test, but perhaps none of these hardships can compare to another storm that Anna had to overcome.

When Anna was thirty-three years old, her husband Henry's behavior began to change. He became unhappy and angry; eventually, he'd turn violent toward her and the children. Then he began to simply walk away from the farm at night, wandering until a neighbor would find him and bring him home. Next, he began to have trouble controlling the movement of his arms and shoulders—they'd jerk wildly.

After years of confusion, it was discovered that Henry had developed an unusual and fatal neurologic disease called Huntington's chorea. Anna learned that there was no treatment for this condition. What's more, she discovered that each of her eight children had a 50 percent chance of developing the same disease. Henry eventually became bedridden and needed constant care as he deteriorated; thus, the oldest son, my father, had to quit school after the eighth grade and assume the task of running the farm with his mother's help.

Henry died after fifteen years of suffering, while his younger kids were still in school. Over the next forty years, Anna would witness the onset and death of five of their eight children from Huntington's chorea. In a final quirk of fate, my father, who had served as the head of the family, was later diagnosed with early-onset Alzheimer's disease. He too passed away prematurely.

My grandmother lived through some of the most difficult times in the history of America. She witnessed the death of most of her children and her only husband. But she was not a weak woman. She did what most of us hope we would do in those circumstances: She rose above her trials, coped with her misfortune, and held her head up with pride. Grandma Moritz relied on her faith and her family to draw strength and hope. When there was enough rain and the price of wheat was high, she was happy. She stayed involved in her extended family, writing letters, and making wedding quilts for every grandchild.

At her one hundreth birthday party, I asked Grandma to tell me something important that she remembered from her youth. She looked at me and immediately replied, "I can remember when Orville and Wilbur [Wright] took off! I was in the second grade." At that same party, the mayor gave her the keys to the city. She held up the oversized wooden key and said, "Does this work at the bank?" Her sense of humor remained quite intact!

Some people do break in the storm, but Grandma Moritz was a role model for my family to be strong and to overcome life's cruel troubles. She died on December 24, 1999, at 103 years old!

Grandma Rust

If you were born in a small farming community, as I was, you can maybe remember how those communities could produce some very unique individuals. My grandma Rust was a one-of-a-kind lady whom I'll never forget—after all, she usually drove around in her big green Chrysler with an open whiskey bottle and cooler within reach! After she died, my entire inheritance consisted of an old dried-out coconut! A woman like that deserves to be remembered. Let me tell you about her.

Audrey Eiler was the eldest of three girls born on a small farm in the breaks of the Missouri River in South Dakota. Their place was located near Fort Randall. The US Army had abandoned this fort two years before Custer's defeat at the Little Big Horn. As sodbusters, the Eiler family lived in a clapboard house half dug into the ground and roofed with dirt and grass. Her mother, Catherine, died early on from complications of lupus disease. Not an easy beginning for little Audrey.

Audrey's father, William, was of Scots–Irish ancestry. He was a farmer, horse trader, square dance caller, bootlegger, and hard drinker. He was abusive to his wife, and my grandmother never forgave him for that. I can remember being afraid of the old guy, but he would sometimes buy us kids an ice cream cone at the local pool hall. He served time in the federal prison at Fort Leavenworth, Kansas, for selling moonshine to the Lakota Indians during the mid-thirties.

Audrey's life changed at a square dance that her father was calling. She met Frank Rust at a Saturday evening dance in Herrick, South Dakota. Frank was a hardworking farmer who owned land with his father just outside of town. Audrey switched her religion from Methodist to Catholic, and they married, then raised a family on the farm. Their last child, Jimmy, died when he ingested sweetened grain that had been poisoned for grasshopper control, but Audrey's other five children were healthy, and they grew into adulthood.

In 1945, Audrey and Frank left the farm and moved into town. At that time, Herrick had about two hundred citizens. The town board decided to operate a municipally owned liquor outlet, so they converted an old bank building into a liquor store. Audrey and Frank were hired to run it.

In between customers, Audrey would throw coal into the potbellied stove and sew clothing. She was a really good seamstress! While most other women used the simpler Butterick or Simplicity patterns, she sewed with the fancier Vogue patterns.

During our annual visits to Herrick, Grandma would teach us kids a thing or two about the liquor business. We could each calculate the alcohol content of a bottle from its proof. I could even make her a dry martini by the time I was twelve years old!

If you ran the only place to buy hard liquor in town, you had the right to consider yourself part of the elite of Herrick. Grandma Rust didn't pass up on that opportunity, so she played the role of the grand dame to the fullest! Audrey dressed well, drove fancy cars, stayed politically active, and maintained the best-kept house in town. There were plenty of chickens in the coop out back of the house, and there was a well-tended vegetable and flower garden there, too.

Audrey smoked too many Camel cigarettes, so she developed a heart condition, but before dying, she bought a trailer house in Arizona and spent more than just a bit of time gambling in Las Vegas. Maybe that's why I inherited only that old coconut! But if living well is the best revenge, Grandma Rust's life ended better than it began. She was a woman who developed her own incomparable style, and I will always remember her for it!

It Is Difficult to Judge

One advantage of being an eye doctor is that I see many patients representing a broad array of occupations. This gives me the opportunity to pick the brains of skilled electricians, plumbers, farmers, and others. I can learn a lot about things that are helpful to me. There are two kinds of patients that I am especially careful around, though: policemen and judges. After all, if I run into one of those guys outside my office, it probably means trouble!

I have been in court twice because of traffic tickets. In both cases, I believed that there were special circumstances showing my innocence. Each time, the judge overruled my excuses and threw the book at me—full fines just like anyone else! This is not to say that all of my interactions with judges have been negative.

Informal advice gleaned from a couple of federal bankruptcy judges passing through my examining room has kept me on the straight and narrow!

Speaking of federal judges, I even have one in the family. My cousin, Nancy Moritz, was appointed by President Obama to serve as judge for the United States Court of Appeals, Tenth Circuit. The US Senate confirmed her, and I recently attended her investiture. Quite the scene! Four hundred guests, and all but a few were judges or attorneys. There were even federal agents with bomb-sniffing dogs! How did my cousin manage to leave the rest of my family in the dust and attain such an important position? Well, it wasn't because she was born with a silver spoon in her mouth—after all, she was a Moritz, just like the rest of us.

Our grandparents were farmers living near a town of 400 people called Tipton, Kansas. On the surface, that sounds unremarkable, but the truth is they never owned any land, for they were only sharecroppers. Having eight children to feed was sometimes more than they could manage. To make matters worse, my grandfather developed Huntington's disease, and he died in the prime of life.

My grandparents' fifth son was named Louis. Louis served as a telephone lineman in the army during the Korean War. After the war, he married a young deaf woman named Carol and became the postmaster in Tipton. Louis and Carol had six children in the short span of five years. Their fourth child was a girl named Nancy.

When Nancy was seven years old, her father, too, was diagnosed with Huntington's disease. His symptoms eventually became so severe that he had to be hospitalized. Carol then moved the family from Tipton to Salina, where there would be work opportunities. All the kids had to work to make ends meet, so Nancy took on work as a hotel desk clerk during her high school years. Despite long hours on the job, she excelled in debate and got very good grades. During those years, Nancy also had to contend with painful and emotional family visits to the VA hospital, watching her dad slowly die from an incurable disease.

Scholarships and low-income grants enabled Nancy to attend both college and law school. She had work-study jobs and full-time summer jobs. During law school, she even worked as a clerk for county judges. Her ability to speak, write, and interpret the law led to public appointments as a judge. Eventually, she served as a Kansas Supreme Court justice.

Now as a federal judge, this exceptional cousin could be just one step away from serving on the US Supreme Court! My siblings and I continue to follow Nancy's career as a judge. We're proud of her, and we are proud of her family's role in shaping such an exceptional woman.

The other day, a lawyer named Tom returned for an eye examination. I walked in and shook his hand, asking, "What's new with you, Tom?"

He smiled broadly as he said, "The governor has just appointed me to be a judge!" After congratulating him, we then got down to the business at hand. I instructed him to watch an eye chart through the Phoroptor. Then I said, "Tom, I am going to show you those letters two ways. Please tell me which way is better. This is number one, and this is number two."

Tom hesitated. Finally, he reluctantly said, "I don't know— it's difficult to judge." *Indeed*, I thought, *it is difficult to judge*. In fact, it can be very difficult to become a judge! Just ask my cousin Nancy!

Geronimo!

I jumped out of an airplane the other day. Now, I did not come by this decision lightly or quickly. In fact, I began thinking about jumping when I was in basic training for the Army. Back then, two big sergeants walked up to another kid and me. I was the smallest guy in the platoon, and the other guy was the largest. They tried to talk us into going airborne and becoming paratroopers. I remember asking, "Would we each get the same size parachute?" The answer was yes, one size fits all. I may not have been too bright, but having the wrong size parachute didn't sound good to me, so I passed on that opportunity.

So there I was a few days ago, sitting 15,000 feet in the air, with my legs hanging out of an airplane door. My instructor was counting up to three, and I was about to take the plunge. Do you know what was on my mind? I was thinking about paratroopers inhabiting my past. (No, not that pair of Army sergeants!) You see, I come from a short line of paratroopers—a line of two, to be exact. Let me tell you about them.

My uncle Harry was a great guy! Tall, lean, always tan and hardened from Kansas fieldwork, he used to grab us kids by one leg and carry us upside down! Then he would play tricks on us with matches or playing cards. He was so strong that he could crush a steel beer can between his thumb and forefinger. Harry drove a red Ford convertible. Man, that was a cool car!

Harry joined the Army between the wars. He was a crack rifle shot and went on to teach marksmanship. He also qualified as a paratrooper by making five jumps—this at a time when being a military paratrooper was a very dangerous occupation. Soldiers were killed in training, and the missions they went on were some of the toughest in war. As a boy, I asked Uncle Harry what it was like to jump out of an airplane. He answered, "It helps if you're not too smart. Otherwise, you would never jump."

Harry was a member of the 101st Airborne Division when he left the Army. Returning to his hometown in Kansas, he ran a small restaurant that had a one-lane bowling alley in the back. I got paid a nickel for every line of bowling when I set the pins. You see, there wasn't an automatic pinsetter; we did it by hand.

As Harry grew into his thirties, he began to show symptoms of Huntington's chorea; an arm would suddenly twitch or he would fall down. His father had died of this genetic disease, and Harry was given the same diagnosis during a visit to the veterans hospital in Topeka. Harry was a fighter and despised his situation, so he kept working and driving well beyond when he should have stopped. Eventually, he was admitted to the hospital where he lived until his death at age forty-three. Uncle Harry's military tombstone has an image of a parachute etched into it.

The other paratrooper in my family came from my mother's side. My cousin Mike Schlegelmilch and I were born exactly one year apart. Mike was one tough kid! He had a hard time in school, but he played on the football team. I can remember his knees swelling up from sports injuries. Mike wasn't college material, so after high school, he joined the Army. With Vietnam going on, the Army took him and even let him go into the 82nd Airborne Division despite his knees.

After we both finished our stints in the Army, I paid Mike a visit in South Dakota. When we talked about jumping, I asked him if it was scary the first time and if subsequent jumps became easier. "Just the opposite," he said. "The first time, you don't know how dangerous it is. Then with each jump, the fear gets worse—much worse!" He said that too many closely packed soldiers coming down together was crazy! Mike then went on to describe a jump that could have been catastrophic.

Shortly after leaving the plane, a lieutenant landed on top of Mike's open parachute! Then, when the other soldier walked off of Mike's 'chute, they got tangled together, face to face. The panicking officer then wanted to open his reserve 'chute. In spite of his own terror, Mike remembered from training that that would collapse both parachutes and then they would have nothing. The lieutenant insisted and kept trying to open his reserve 'chute, but Mike slugged him in the face a couple of times on the way down!

Mike's tough ways continued after he was discharged. He took on two guys in a bar fight and ended up in a veterans hospital with severe head trauma. He worked as a church janitor until he had a series of seizures. Mike died in that VA hospital at age thirty-seven.

Well, the last thing I heard before my jump was "Three!" Out I went! What was it like? Brutal and terrifying! When the wind hit my face at 180 miles an hour, I thought my cheeks were going to get torn off! And I had forgotten that at nearly three miles up, it could be darn cold, even in July. During the sixty-second free fall, I tried to look anywhere but down. I could hear the parachute popping open, and I hung on to my straps for dear life! I was surprised my feet didn't keep going. I executed a "perfect" landing—no broken bones. Would I jump again? No way! Enough is plenty!

The other two paratroopers in my family both had shortened lives, each ending in a veterans hospital. We had all served in the military, and now we had each jumped out of an airplane. It makes me smile when I think of each of them parachuting for the first time!

The Kansas Boys

At the end of World War II, my father had left the military and needed a job. His brothers had taken over the chores on their Kansas farm, so Dad and three other young men moved north to South Dakota. They found farm work around the very small, mostly German, town of Herrick. To this day, those four men are still known in Herrick as "the Kansas boys." I lost track of two of them (Arnold Mick and one of the Thummel brothers), but I know the fates of the other two were played out on the same farm.

My father, Norbert Moritz, started working as a farmhand for Frank Rust. Soon, he married Frank's daughter, and then Frank gave him the chance to run the family farm. My parents started raising their children while they planted about eighty acres of crops. We had pigs, chickens, and three cows. We were what you might call subsistence farmers. My parents were just trying to work the land to put food on the table and survive! These were hard times, and a lack of rain for three years in a row eventually forced us off the farm. Some of my earliest memories

BERT MORITZ

came from living on that place. Let me tell you about those experiences.

Sitting in the middle of the flat, desolate prairie was our white wood-framed farmhouse. It had always struck me as odd that the house had so many small bedrooms upstairs and such a large eating space downstairs. I didn't understand that until years later, when my parents explained to me that the house had been built not as a farmhouse but as a sanitarium (hospital)! A physician had constructed the building at the turn of the last century for patients who had tuberculosis. He had wanted them isolated from the rest of the population, and what better place for that than South Dakota!

With four kids running around the place and lots of farm chores to do, my mother did not always keep a close eye on us. Once, I wandered about a mile down the gravel road until I came to the highway. A Lakota woman named Rain Water stopped her car, picked me up, and drove me back home. Mom was grateful to Rain Water, but she gave me a swat for that one!

We had some big pigs, and Mom worried that the sows might roll over onto the smaller kids. Her strategy was to convince us that the pigs wanted to eat us. She hoped that this would keep us out of the pigpen. It worked! I mentally celebrated the day that Dad brought out his rifle and shot a hog so we could butcher it!

We had a big dog named Shep. When I was about four years old, I was walking across the gravel farmyard and I had a run-in with our dog. Shep was chasing the chickens again. A rooster ran right between my legs, and that dog came right after it! I was flipped over backward and my head landed on a piece of glass. There was probably more screaming than blood coming out of me, but my cut needed stitches. Dad drove me to the doctor. I can still remember the ice cream cone that I got to eat on the way back to the farm.

After we left the farm, my grandfather decided to give another one of the Kansas boys a chance at it. Walt Krier moved into the house and started by working those same eighty acres. He was a good farmer, and eventually, he made a go of it. In fact, over the next thirty years, Walt bought all eight hundred acres!

A couple of years ago, I decided to stop in and see Walt. At ninety years old, he was still working the land with one of his sons. As I drove up the drive in July, I could see that the corn was dried out and that it was ruined. After I shook his hand, I asked him what had happened to his corn. Walt got a sour look on his face and said, "The darn stuff just burned up. The rains were spotty, and we were in the wrong spot!" I knew just how he felt. As his wife, Henrietta, gave us a piece of pie and some coffee, Walt took out his photo album and opened it up on the kitchen table. He proceeded to prove to me that he could boast about something that no other farmer in America could lay claim to. Walt and his wife had flown on Air Force One with three different presidents of the United States! You see, his other son had joined the Secret Service and was in charge of the president's airplane!

When each of those Kansas Boys took his turn at running the farm, he expected to be successful, but hard work isn't always rewarded. My family had to move on to something else, and Walt's family made their stand there. I take pride when I think back to the farm days, and I still keep in touch with Walt Krier.

The Rest of the Story

My uncle Chuck is a hero in our family, and I consider him an American hero too. Here's why...

Along with my father, Chuck had to quit school in the eighth grade to help run the family farm because their father had been stricken with a neurological disease. During World War II, Chuck joined the Navy and served in combat. After his service, he earned a college degree and had a successful career as a Chicago businessman. Chuck is now almost ninety years old, is married to the same woman, and has raised a happy family. A man of great honesty, Chuck would be the first to admit that he has caught a few lucky breaks along the way.

Uncle Chuck told me many years ago that after the war, he had started college at Creighton University in Nebraska because he wanted to become an accountant. During his first semester, however, a course in algebra was required and he knew that this would be trouble! He struggled but just couldn't do the math. Thus, a meeting with the professor was in order.

The meeting started out with a conversation something like this: "Why is it, young man, that you can't do these problems correctly? What don't you understand?"

Chuck said, "I've never seen numbers like this before."

Then the professor asked, "Didn't you pay attention in your high school algebra class?"

Chuck responded, "No, I didn't attend high school."

The professor looked stunned andsaid, "You didn't go to high school! How did you get into this university?"

Chuck answered, "I don't know. I just applied and they let me in."

At this point in the conversation, Chuck knew things could go badly. Would the professor have him expelled? No. Instead, the professor spent some extra time teaching Chuck the math, and he never mentioned it again. That was quite the lucky break for my uncle!

Now let me tell you the rest of the story. I was attending college at St. Cloud State University in Minnesota in 1975. My roommate was an accounting major named Darrell. One day, Darrell mentioned to me he was applying for a job in Chicago at a big company called Jewell Corporation. What a coincidence! I then told him that my uncle was treasurer for the whole corporation. And that was that, I thought.

About a month later, Darrell announced that he had been lucky enough to land an interview for the job. He said that he had put my uncle Chuck's name down on the application as a personal reference. Not only that, but Darrell wanted me to call Chuck and "put in a good word for him" before the interview. Yikes!

I was a bit uncomfortable calling Uncle Chuck and explaining all of this to him. After all, my uncle had never met Darrell, and Chuck could be an intimidating guy! He had two secretaries and a large office with a huge, fancy desk located at the top of a skyscraper near O'Hare Airport. He was always impeccably dressed, well spoken, and not the kind of executive you tried to buffalo about anything.

Nevertheless, I picked up the phone and called Chuck at his office. I explained the situation about Darrell coming for an interview. Chuck stopped me right there and said, "Your friend will not get hired at this corporation. His application will end up in the wastebasket." I was stunned! How could this be? I asked. "We want good accountants who have attended the Harvard or Stanford schools of business. Since he didn't attend either of those colleges, he won't be seriously considered."

I had to think fast to help Darrell. I responded, "Uncle Chuck, do you remember the story you told me about how you got into college without going to high school? And didn't you say that a professor gave you a break and helped you stay in school?

Well, Darrell is a good midwestern hardworking kid just like you were. I think that he deserves a break too."

"That's not going to happen," retorted Chuck, and that was the end of our conversation.

Later, when Darrell asked me if I had put in a good work for him, I just smiled and said, "Uncle Chuck knows that you are coming."

When Darrell returned from his interview in Chicago, he had a big smile on his face. "I got the job!" he said. "And at the end of the interview, they told me that Mr. Charles Moritz had recommended me for the position!"

Well, I was shocked! Had my uncle decided to help Darrell based on our conversation, or had he just been testing me by saying that Darrell would be rejected based on where he had gone to college? Had he really been trying to see if I felt strongly enough to defend Darrell? I never asked, but as the years went by, Uncle Chuck would give me occasional updates on Darrell's career at Jewell Corporation. When Chuck retired, Darrell was still moving up the corporate ladder, just as Chuck had done some thirty years before. Now you know!

Those Magnificent Men
and Their Flying Machines

It's hard to comprehend how fast things are changing. I remember talking to Grandma Moritz about some of her best memories. She was born in 1896, and she was one hundred years old at the time of our conversation. "Tell me something important that you remember, Grandma." I said. She smiled and exclaimed with a twinkle in her eye, "Oh, I can remember when I was in the second grade and Orville and Wilbur [Wright] took off." Wow! Now that had an impact on me. Imagine what she had experienced during her lifetime, just in flight alone!

Coming from a family of sharecroppers in Kansas, my father, Norbert, had plenty of time for hard work and little time for pleasure, but he could dream—and his dream was to fly! I can imagine him looking up from the wheat fields into that blue and cloudless sky to watch the rare sight of a passing airplane. When a traveling air show would come through, he would see the twisting stunt planes with their fearless wing walkers thrilling the crowd. These were my dad's heroes. This was who he wanted to be. He could not have known then that it would take a world war to get him off the ground!

After the attack on Pearl Harbor, America needed pilots, and it needed them in a hurry! My dad tried to enlist in the Army Air Corps, but he had to wait two years until his younger brothers were old enough to run the farm. Then he needed to pass the physical. I remember Dad telling me that he was afraid that he would be too short to qualify as a pilot so the day of his physical, he did pull-ups with weights attached to his ankles! It must have worked, because he was accepted.

There were no openings in any flight-training programs, however, so Dad was told to study at home. I still have the home training manual that he used. It has mostly simple drawings like a comic book, with captions reading: "To gain altitude, pull back on the stick. To lose altitude, push forward on the stick." Arrows in the diagrams indicated the airplane going up or down. (Things were a lot simpler in those days!) After a few months of home study, Dad finally got into the Army and up into the air!

Like all the other young guys back then, Norbert wanted to be a hotshot fighter pilot. But fate wouldn't have it, as his eyes began to change. Thus, he was washed out of the fighter program and then put into glider training! Once again, his luck failed, because after D-Day, the Army's glider program was discontinued. Not needed, he was eventually sent back to the Kansas farm fields.

Finding himself at home and grounded again, he would not be deterred, for he had had a taste of flying, so at the end of the war, Dad and a friend scraped together enough cash to buy an Army surplus airplane called an Aeronca Champ. This was a small red tail dragger made from doped linen stretched over a wooden frame. It wasn't much, but it was his!

One of my earliest memories in life is sitting on my father's lap in that Aeronca, watching a wooden stick slowly move forward and back. We were flying over our farm, with the rest of the family watching from below. Suddenly, Dad gunned the engine and pulled the stick sharply. We leaned back, and then to my amazement, I was hanging upside down! Afterward, I recall landing in the pasture out back of the house. I'm surprised that my second memory in life is not hearing my mother give Dad heck for flying so crazy with my brother and me onboard!

Every Fourth of July, Dad would buzz low over town and then climb straight up until the plane stalled. It would then tumble backward, appearing out of control and heading toward the ground until he pulled it out of the stall just at the last moment. He called that maneuver "hammer handle."

Norbert knew that he needed to make some money with his airplane in order to keep it, so he and his buddy tried crop-dusting, but the plane crashed in a bean field, and Mom put her foot down—he had to sell his share.

Flying was still in Dad's blood, so some years later, he became a volunteer for the Civil Air Patrol. In those days, there were no black boxes or transponders to help locate a missing airplane. Dad would be notified of a downed aircraft, and he would fly over the search area, looking for wreckage and survivors.

Once, Dad rented a small airplane and I came along on his flight to Canton, South Dakota. After an uneventful flight, we landed on a bumpy grass landing strip. When it came time to leave, he pointed out a grove of tall trees at the end of the runway. As we began our rollout for take-off, he warned me that we might not be able to get enough ground speed to clear those trees. Well, we came so close to those trees that I could have picked an apple! I think that he was just trying to scare me (again!).

Dad and a couple of other pilots got together and tried to buy another airplane, but by this time late in his life, aircraft were just too expensive, so he couldn't make it work, and then he developed Alzheimer's disease at age sixty-two, so his flying days were over. As I drove him to the nursing home, he looked up and saw a single-engine airplane flying overhead. With a wistful look, he said to me, "I wish I could have just a couple more hours up there."

I still have Dad's wings insignia and the logbook documenting each hour that he flew. My brother Dave built a scale model of an Aeronca Champ and painted it red. At our family reunions, those magnificent men in their flying machines are well remembered, and with much pride!

Staying Put

Relatives on both sides of my family had three things in common. First, they didn't have much money. Second, they had to work hard to get by. Finally, they were all stubborn Germans. The Moritzes down in Kansas sharecropped land and grew wheat. The Rusts out in South Dakota began as sodbusters and raised corn.

It took me a while to figure out just how stubborn our German ancestors were. Both families not only lived through the Dust Bowl but also stayed on their farms. This was at a time when literally hundreds of thousands of families had the good sense to abandon the prairie land and head west to California. That decision to stay on the land had an impact on every family member, even the youngest.

I can remember standing on the edge of a small lake near Herrick, South Dakota, while talking to Grandpa Rust. He explained to me that the lake was artificial and that he had helped dig it during the Great Depression. It was a WPA project. I could see that there was a large earthen dam that they had put in to hold the water. "Did you use those big-old steam shovels?" I asked.

Grandpa just looked at me and said, "No, we used horses, wagons, and hand shovels." He should have added copious amounts of backbone and elbow grease to that list!

On the land that my dad's family farmed in Kansas, there was a pond for the cows and pigs. Dad told me that he and his father used a scraper and their horse to build what he said was "the biggest earthen dam in the state of Kansas when we got it done." I didn't know if he was pulling my leg about that, but I knew enough not to ask if he and his dad used a steam shovel!

When Dad told me about the "Dirty Thirties," he always included descriptions of the great dust clouds rolling over the plains toward their Kansas farm. They knew that more dust was going to foul the machinery, cover the dinner plates, and stick in their lungs, "but nothing was worse," he said, "than when the clouds were filled not with dust but with grasshoppers!" Oh, how they hated those insects! Millions came, darkening the day and covering everything. They ate the laundry on the line, the paint off the house, and, worst of all, the wheat growing in the fields. And after the grasshoppers came hunger. I finally understood how bad it was when I learned that the family's youngest child, Francis, was diagnosed with malnutrition at age three.

South Dakota had fewer dust storms, but times were tough there too. Often, a promising crop was ruined by drought—and the grasshoppers came there, too, for they could eat corn just as well as wheat! Grandpa Rust recalled that he had kept grain treated with poison and sorghum on hand for grasshopper control—anything to kill the hoppers before the fields were stripped bare! Farming has always been dangerous, however. Their youngest of six kids, Jimmy, was so hungry that they caught him eating that tainted grain right out of the bag!

After that hard upbringing, my Uncle Francis went on to be a sergeant in the army and fight in the Korean War. He carried a machine gun into one of the worst battles of the war and was given a Bronze Star for bravery. Twenty years later, he died in a Kansas veterans hospital. Francis had inherited Huntington's chorea.

What became of little Jimmy Rust? That young child's fate was worse. He died at age four from eating that poisoned grain. Grandpa felt so bad that he never talked about Jimmy again.

It's easy to think of my relatives as a bunch of stubborn Germans. Maybe they were never the sharpest tools in the box, but they helped build this country by not giving up and by not abandoning their way of life. With the decision to stay came sacrifice. No one ever quit; no one ever left. They lived by the land, and they died by the land.

Uncle Chuck and Aunt Natalie

I had just returned from a Moritz family reunion in Tipton, Kansas. My uncle Chuck was the oldest living member of the clan, and that year, we had celebrated his ninetieth birthday. He hit the ceremonial first golf ball at the tournament. Afterward, during the Saturday night dinner, a local elderly woman sat at Chuck's table. As a friend of the family, she was asked to say a few words about him. We were all quite surprised to hear that as a young woman, she had hoped to catch the eye of that tall, handsome lad from a nearby farm, but instead, Chuck had fancied another girl—a girl named Natalie.

After Chuck's discharge from the Navy at the end of World War II, he and Natalie were married. Thus they began their journey through life together. His life's work found expression in the business world, culminating as a successful executive at a large company in Chicago. Natalie's contribution came through the raising of three children, and other work outside the home. Having accomplished all of this, together, they built a lakeside retirement home in Wisconsin. They grew old together quite happily.

Chuck has always been quick-witted and good with language. One Christmas while he was still working, his secretary gave him a present—a book titled *A Book of Poems*. When Chuck opened it, he discovered that every page was empty, and so he took the hint and began to write his own poetry.

Natalie is a slim, very pretty woman who has a special grace. She is strong-willed, enjoys gardening, and likes cooking healthy foods. She has a deep faith and is active in her church.

Some of Chuck's most touching poems are about Natalie and their life's journey together. Here are two poems about their marriage.

MARRIAGE VOWS

Limited choices;
Perilous plight.
Angelic voices;
You got it right!

I DO. DO YOU?

Motives for marriage
can vary a lot.
Some seem both foolish
and funny.
One thing I'll say for
this soul mate I've got:
She sure didn't marry
for money.

We all know that marriage is not easy. An ability to compromise and to adjust to the unexpected is a minimum requirement. Uncle Chuck is often heard saying, "Life is one long lesson in humility." His words never rang truer than three years before this party, when Natalie was diagnosed with dementia. Here are two poems that he wrote in response to her illness:

EARLY ONSET

First thing this morning
She ventured to say:
"The house I was born in
is slipping away."

ADVICE FOR A CERTAIN CAREGIVER

Brain "derailment"?
It will worsen.
Blame the ailment,
Not the person.

Thus, they sold their beautiful home on the lake and moved into a care facility near Milwaukee. As Natalie's condition worsened, she had to move into an Alzheimer's unit. Chuck maintains his own room and visits her twice daily. They still have dinner together every evening.

In years past, my aunt and uncle served as an example for me. Their lives became my definition of success: life in the suburbs, a healthy family, a loving marriage, and a quiet retirement. But now, under adversity, they have become even more of an inspiration. As Natalie's disease advances, Chuck remains unwavering in his love for her.

Chuck wrote this last poem for their recent anniversary:

DEAR NATALIE

In all kinds of weather,
Midst laughter, midst tears,
We've now been together
For sixty-three years.
I've said it before:
"You're never a bore."
So let's sign the contract
For year sixty-four.

Part Four—Friends

There is nothing better than a friend—unless it is a friend with chocolate.

—Linda Grayson

What a complicated society we live in. We have to interact with a variety of people, whether we want to or not: our colleagues at work, family members, the in-laws, people at the grocery store, that guy who won't stop talking in the movie theater, and on and on it goes! There is one exception to this rule of unintended interaction: friends.

I've gotten to choose my friends, and after a lifetime of choosing, I think that I have done quite well. The beauty of friendship is that no relationship needs to be a bad one. If something goes awry, we can just terminate the relationship and move on to another. Try that with your boss and you'll likely be reading the help-wanted ads in your local newspaper.

The following stories illustrate that each of us has a wide variety of friends. Mine include childhood acquaintances, high school buddies, senior citizens, and, of course, man's best friend. Now, don't think that I have had an abundance of friends. I have not. Moving from town to town taught me to form friendships readily, yet it guaranteed those bonds would be easily broken. All of the friends mentioned in these stories are out of my life now. But their memories make me smile. Maybe that's the definition of true friendship.

The Best Dog Ever

When you live on a farm, you don't necessarily think of animals as pets. After all, most of them are going to end up on someone's dinner table! We always had a dog, but we didn't play with it much. Our dog spent most of its time chasing chickens around the barnyard. We also had too many cats. Born in the darkest corners of the barn, the kittens seemed expendable. A tomcat might kill them just after birth, or they would get run over by the tractor. In the winter, the cats had an unfortunate habit of sitting on top of our car's front tires. It was warm near the engine, but this was a poor choice that often proved fatal for the cats when Dad drove to town.

After we left the farm, I began to look at animals in a whole new way. They became pets and, in some ways, part of our family. While growing up, we had several housedogs, but it seemed we just couldn't avoid problems. Our collie, named Shep, drowned in an abandoned farm well. A delightful water spaniel (also named Shep) was hit by a car. We just couldn't get a Dalmatian named Buckshot house-trained, so he ended up living in South Dakota with my grandmother. We always had a few turtles in shoeboxes, fish swimming in bowls, and jars full of frogs or insects. A family favorite was a yellow parakeet we called Sammy. I liked to let it out of the cage when the folks weren't looking. One day, I forgot to close the front door of the house, and that was the last we ever saw of Sammy! But the best pet that I ever had was a little white dog named Eddy.

When my daughter was ten years old, she insisted on getting a puppy. I wasn't comfortable with having a dog in the house, so I tried to placate her with a large turtle. She named it Shelly, but then she let me know that my ploy had failed: "You can't play with a turtle! I need a puppy." I dutifully fed Shelly worms and cleaned the turtle cage weekly for the next twelve years. At one point, I considered starting a college savings account for that animal. Finally, it expired.

Not long after my failed ploy to substitute a turtle for Anna's puppy yearning, we answered a newspaper ad that announced "Shi Tzu Puppies for Sale." We all drove to the small town of Cameron, Wisconsin. An older gentleman showed us two energetic balls of fur. Anna chose the one she deemed the cuter, and so we had a new member of the family! With the exception of a mild heart murmur, he appeared to be a perfect pup. Anna considered several names for the dog but eventually settled on Eddy.

From the onset, it was apparent that this was one smart dog. During house-training, I built a makeshift fence to keep Eddy off the carpet, but every time I turned around, he had easily outsmarted me and was running on the carpet! Then he developed an odd habit at dinnertime. Rather than just eating after we filled the food bowl, Eddy would first scratch on the nearby clothes dryer with his paw. Then I had to walk over and tap on his bowl before he would chow down. It became apparent that he was asking permission to eat. Soon, Eddy learned that repeating this ritual enough times earned him a scrap of meat from our dinner table!

It is common for us dog owners to believe that our little friends can talk to us and understand everything we say. Eddy seemed quite adept at accurately interpreting our vocalized questions and commands; however, he also learned to vary the tone of his bark to convey his need to go outside or his desire to ride in the car, or to request a well-deserved treat. When it was time to play, he would bump my leg or toss a toy at my feet. He even learned to yawn loudly when he wanted me to stop reading and offer him some attention.

Eddy had an overly inflated self-image, at least for a dog that never weighed more than seventeen pounds. I am certain that when he looked in the mirror, he must have seen a huge African lion looking back! At obedience class, he fearlessly challenged dogs multiple times his size. If he spotted a deer at the edge of our yard, he would charge into the woods in hot pursuit! There were many times when either Susie or I, clad in only our pajamas, had to dash through the brush to bring that wild guy back.

For such a small dog, Eddy was very tough. A few years back, he became quite sick. The vet diagnosed Eddy with a fungus that had infected his skin and lungs. He warned us that dogs often die from this infection despite treatment, but after lots of pills, Eddy regained his good health. Then, just when things were going well, a large pit bull confronted Eddy in the street. As expected, Eddy didn't back down, and a fight ensued. Puncture wounds on the head, bleeding ears, and a torn-up face proved that he lost that battle, but after many stitches, our Eddy was back into form, none the worse for the wear!

Ah, but being tough is no guarantee of immortality. Remember that heart murmur? Not long ago, Eddy was uncharacteristically short of energy and stopped playing. After fourteen years of active use, his heart had enlarged and was beginning to fail. More medicine from the veterinary office only seemed to delay the inevitable. No longer able to go on walks, he was carried on outings. He also got extra treats. An occasional bowl of ice cream at Dairy Queen was one way we thanked him for being such a great dog!

Though he is gone now, I can say that Eddy was most different from all the other pets that we had. He gave our family years of love and happiness. He is now part of our permanent memory, and he can never be replaced. Eddy was more than man's best friend... He was the best dog ever!

Doug

Farming in South Dakota was a tough way to scrounge out a living in the 1950s and '60s; however, there was one commodity that was never in short supply—pheasants! Those beautiful birds were everywhere! You might therefore expect my best memories of pheasant hunting to be from South Dakota, but there is one experience in Iowa that I cherish most, and it included my good friend Doug.

Doug Mooney was a guy my brother Dave and I hung around with in high school. Doug was taller than me, and good-looking. At the time, we lived in the farming community of Estherville, Iowa. As you might imagine, the countryside around there was mainly flat cornfields, with almost no forests or rivers. That geography didn't slow Doug down when it came to his aspirations, however. He wanted to be, more than anything else, a true sportsman. He read magazines like *Field and Stream* and *Outdoor Life* to learn about nature and to know how to behave in the great outdoors.

Doug was very particular with his sporting equipment. Rather than buy a canoe, he made his own version from wood and fiberglass. Once, when he and I were paddling down the muddy Des Moines River, we hit a submerged tree branch and tore a gaping hole in the canoe's side. As the water poured in and we headed for the shore, I began to wonder if this was the way the crew of the *Titanic* felt!

Doug imposed on himself a hunting code of ethics that was more restrictive than the law required. He was a one-shot hunter partly because he had lost his shotgun's magazine on a duck hunt one fall. He refused to replace it, preferring to hunt with the handicap. His ethics also included eating every animal he shot. He simply felt it was senseless to kill an animal for no reason. One time, though, I tried a bite of his rabbit stew. The taste was awful; I began to wonder if Doug knew salt from pepper!

I did some time overseas when I was in the Army. When I went back to Estherville in January for rest and relaxation, I gave Doug a call just to see what he was up to. Doug told me he had a girlfriend named Rhonda and that he was taking a course in auto body repair. He mentioned that Iowa had a special pheasant-hunting season that year. It was a bitterly cold day outside and there was deep snow on the ground, but we decided to go hunting anyway and ended up having a lot of fun. After that hunt, Doug and I shook hands and parted, not knowing that we'd never see each other again.

Twelve years later, when Susan and I were living in Altoona, the telephone rang; it was Doug on the line! Imagine how surprised and happy I was that he'd called me! We talked at length, swapping stories about our lives and adventures since we'd last met. Doug explained that he had married Rhonda and they had two children: Phillip, age five, and Christine, age two. He'd landed a nice job in Estherville at the Chevy garage as an auto body repairman.

I then asked about his parents, and he took me by surprise when he said, "Why, they are right here with me in my room." He went on to explain, "I'm in a hospital at Mayo Clinic in Rochester. I have been getting treatment for leukemia, but they are out of treatment options. Mom and Dad are here to take me home for the last time." I was completely stunned, and I didn't know what to say! He seemed resolved to his fate, and that gave me some strength to do the best I could as our conversation wound down, but still, it was a sad end to a wonderful conversation and likely end to a great friendship. Two weeks later, I got word that Doug had died at the age of thirty-three. I mourned the loss of a very good man.

Five years ago my brother Dave took a drive down to Iowa. He looked up Doug's two children and met with them. Dave told the kids stories about our adventures as high school classmates. He wanted them to know what their father was like. Now whenever I think about Doug, I visualize our last hunt together.

> *Making our way through rows of snow-covered picked corn, I looked to my left. Just then, a pheasant exploded out of the field right at Doug's feet! He shouldered his shotgun. He took his time, waiting until the bird was farther out. Then he slowly squeezed the trigger. It was a perfect, clean shot! As Doug bent down and scooped up the bird from the sparkling snow, he looked at me. He gave me a thumbs-up and a beaming smile.*

Hilmar Mostul

Abraham Lincoln once said, "The better part of my life has been my friendships." When Susan and I moved to Eau Claire in 1982, I didn't have a single friend in town. I was unhappy and wasn't at all certain that we were going to stay, but all of that changed with a chance meeting one day. Who knew that my life would be so influenced?

Work at my new office had been very slow, with few patients. I had too much time on my hands, so one day, I put my fishing poles in the car and headed for the Eau Claire River. Near the Highway K Bridge north of Fall Creek was a pretty area, so I began to fish there. Shortly after I started, an older man came walking past. We had a short conversation, and then he continued his walk down the river. I noticed that he seemed bored, so I called to him and asked if he would like to fish with me. "Yes, but I don't have a fishing pole," he replied, so I offered him an extra one that I had in the car.

On his first cast, he fouled the line and had a mess on his hands! I cut the line, restrung the pole, and then gave him a quick lesson in casting. As you might expect, we managed to learn a lot about each other while fishing together that day. Hilmar Mostul was a recently retired Lutheran minister from Menomonie. He and his wife, Alice, had just moved into a small condominium on the north side of Eau Claire. He felt a bit unsure about living there and, like me, had to find something to do with his extra time. I remarked that the pastor was switching from being a fisher of men to becoming a fisher of fish. Hilmar smiled at that notion. At the end of the day, we had only one small walleye on the stringer, so we let it go.

This chance meeting along the river began a long friendship between our families. He and Alice became de facto grandparents for our daughter. We spent the holidays together, had them over for dinner often, and, at the end of their lives, helped to care for them, but the majority of the relationship between Hilmar and me developed along the hiking and fishing trails. Let me tell you about one particular adventure that we had.

Early one October, we loaded our camping gear into the car and drove up north. After we rented a canoe, the outfitter dropped us off along the Namekogon River. Our plan was to spend three days and two nights boating and fishing our way back to the outfitter's place. What a beautiful river, and what a pleasant time we were having! For two days, we had a warm October sun on our backs and great camping. Then the weather changed. On the second night, the wind shifted and the temperature dropped. Rain, driven by the night's north wind, came under our tent; we awoke in wet, cold sleeping bags.

Unable to get a campfire started, we decided to paddle downstream, but the friendly creek we had paddled the day before was now a rushing torrent that threatened to capsize us! About noon, with Hilmar in the bow of the canoe and me in the stern, we came to our first series of rocks. With the rains pounding hard, this would be a rapids to test our skills. "We'll need to paddle hard to make it through without hitting the rocks!" I shouted. Bending our backs and pulling hard, we came through in fine shape.

Hilmar raised his paddle over his head and exclaimed, "Praise the Lord!"

A bit farther down the river, we encountered another rapids. With white water threatening to swamp our boat again, we again steered carefully and managed to make it through. Raising his paddle, the good pastor again proclaimed, "Praise the Lord!"

Looking ahead, I could see that the river was starting to narrow and that the current was speeding up. There was a sharp bend to the left, and I could hear the water surging against unseen rocks that would soon threaten our passage. This gave me a bad feeling, and my fears were confirmed as we rounded the bend. We were mercilessly swept toward a roaring rapids thickly lined with boulders, and I could see no easy path through them. "Hold on, hold on!" I shouted. The bow of the canoe suddenly rammed a rock, and then the current instantly turned our boat sideways in the river. As the canoe tipped over, Hilmar flipped right out into the torrent of water. Without his weight, the canoe then popped upright and I found myself heading downstream backward! I could see the seventy-two-year-old pastor up to his armpits in freezing, rushing water and knew there wasn't going to be any "Praise the Lord" this time around!

Walking the canoe back upstream against the torrent and using the rocks for footholds, I managed to get back to my friend and help him back in. Hilmar was shaking so much that he couldn't speak. I was worried about him, and I knew that he needed to be warmed up quickly. We drifted downstream until I saw an abandoned bridge abutment along the riverbank. Pulling over, we tried to start a fire, but we had no luck.

I realized that there must be an old road that the bridge had served. Leaving Hilmar and hiking down the abandoned roadway, I came to a highway. I managed to thumb a ride back to the outfitter's place. The outfitter and I returned in a truck and took Hilmar to the nearest town.

In town, Hilmar and I rented a motel room for a while. I put him in a hot tub and took his clothes to a laundromat. You should have seen the smile on his face when he was dressed in warm clothes fresh out of the dryer!

With our gear stowed in the car, we drove south toward home that evening. As we got close, Hilmar turned to me and said, "You can't tell my wife about this at all. If she found out that I'd fallen out of the canoe, I would never get to go again!" We both had a good laugh, and we both kept our mouths shut. Alice never knew.

Thus, Susie and I settled in Eau Claire because of an unexpected friendship that I found along a riverbank. To this day, I think of Hilmar and of the adventures that we shared. He taught me many things about the wonders of the Wisconsin outdoors, and about the wonders of a good friendship.

Nathan, Mike, and Steve

My mother died rather young. She had developed emphysema from smoking Camel cigarettes. Mom thought that she would outlive my father, who was diagnosed with Alzheimer's disease at age sixty-two, but it didn't work out that way. After her funeral, I met my brothers and sisters in our parents' trailer house, and we went through their things. You can imagine the scene. We were sad, and we had to choose who took what. My parents had never had much, and now that was quite obvious!

We were trying to decide who wanted Mom's knitting needles when the phone rang. I put the receiver up to my ear and heard a voice that I hadn't heard in thirty years. Suddenly, the sadness of the day melted away.

"Hello, Bert, this is Steve. I am calling because I just read that your mother had died. I want you to know that she was always so nice to the three of us. She was our Cub Scout den mother in Carlisle, Iowa." Talk about a shock to my memory! My mind went back to the small town of Carlisle. An image of my three childhood buddies—Nathan, Mike, and Steve—flashed before me, each boy with a butch haircut and blue Cub Scout shirt. Nathan was a short, Irish-looking kid with red hair and freckles. Mike was tall, thin, and blonde. Steve was always a bit too big and chubby. I spent my childhood summers with those guys, riding our bikes around town, throwing dirt clods at each other, and swimming in a nearby lake all afternoon. It was a happy time in my life that I had thought would never end, but of course it did.

My family left Carlisle for another town in Iowa called Vinton, and I was suddenly pulled away from my friends. This happened to me a lot, for we lived in eight towns before I completed middle school. I never expected to see those guys again, so I started to make new friends, first in Vinton, where we lived for a year, and then in Iowa Falls.

Our family's two-year stay in Iowa Falls ended just as I completed the seventh grade. On moving day, Dad was helping load our furniture into a big truck when a car pulled up to the house. Out came Nathan, Mike, and Steve! Steve's dad had decided to surprise me by bringing them all up for visit, but there I was, moving yet again! The house was empty of furniture, and we were almost ready to leave town, so we talked a little. I started to cry as we said good-bye after their short visit. Steve reminded me, "You are never going to lose the friends that you have, and you will just make more."

I never saw them again after that day. Even as children, we knew that Nathan's dad drank too much and was abusive. Nathan responded by becoming a lawyer; he now lives in Alaska. Mike stayed in that small Iowa town and works as a laborer. Steve now works as a journalist for the *Des Moines Register*. He happened to read my mother's obituary in the newspaper, and thus the phone call.

After that call, my siblings and I continued to divide my parents' things up. It worked out well. No one seemed to care about the things that were important to me, and vice versa. I ended up with my father's beer glass collection and railroad mementos. I still have them. And Steve was right: I still have the memories of my friendship with my three childhood buddies.

Sam

The other day, I was rummaging through some of my old stuff—you know, that box or two of things that all of us have in our basements, filled with all kinds of mementos that no one will ever want after we're gone. In one small container were some old coins. The nicest one of the bunch was an 1888 silver dollar in mint condition. I recall that a boy named Sam Shonkwiler gave one to both my brother Dave and me. I can't remember exactly when he did that, but I know that it was an act of friendship. And how did Dave and I return his friendship? Well...

We were really into science when we were young. My father had some old radio and TV tube testers in the basement. He never made any money with the equipment, but he tried to fix the broken TVs in the neighborhood. Maybe that's how we got started. Our science interests varied from chemistry and physics to engineering, but it seemed like no matter what we did, it always ended up being destructive!

Dave and I wanted to make some gunpowder. Why? I think that it was just a challenge for Dave to see if he could do it. For my part, I wanted to pack some on top of the rockets that I was building. After a session or two at the public library, we had a list of materials that we needed. In those days, it was possible to order chemicals like powdered magnesium and phosphorus by mail and have the postman deliver them to our house. When we had all the supplies on hand, we headed over to Sam's basement—after all, Dave and I had recently been in trouble for manufacturing and igniting hydrogen in our basement. Best to keep a lid on our new activities since Mom and Dad were on high alert!

Standing in front of the workbench, Sam held a glass beaker (in retrospect, not the safest choice) from our chemistry set. He mixed each component while Dave made the measurements and followed the directions that we had written down. I stayed back at what I considered a safe distance. When we had everything in the beaker, we told Sam to stir it up really good. He was using a metal stir rod, and he put some muscle into it. The explosion caught us all by surprise! It wasn't as loud as you might have thought, but to this day, I can still remember the sulfur smell of that burned gunpowder.

When the smoke cleared, my brother just had some shards of glass in his hair. Sam wasn't so lucky. His forehead was bleeding, and we could see bits of glass sticking out of it. Thank goodness that the guy wore eyeglasses! He began to wail loudly, and we had no chance of hiding this from his mother. She hauled him off to the emergency room after giving each of us a look of death that I will never forget! A few months later, Dave and I were still afraid to go back to Sam's house.

After watching a TV show about World War II, I gotten the idea to build a mortar. Dave helped me perfect the design, and we wanted to show it to Sam. We called and had him ride his bicycle to meet us out in the country. I pounded one end of a three-foot length of heavy plumbing pipe into the ground at a forty-five-degree angle. Then I got out an empty beer can and two M-80 firecrackers (these were the largest that we could buy). I filled the beer can about a third of the way with gravel. Dave held one M-80 and a match. I put the other M-80 just inside the can but held it by the fuse. We were ready to go.

Sam had become, rightfully, wary of our experiments. He stood off to the side and refused to handle any explosives. Dave lit the first charge and threw it into the pipe. I counted to three and then lit mine, stuffing the beer can into the pipe as fast as I could. When the first M-80 exploded, it blasted that can right into the air. Then the second one detonated and the can was blasted into pieces! Wow, was that great! Dave and I were about to high-five each other when we looked over at Sam. He looked really pale, and there was blood coming from his knee! Oh no! The poor guy had been hit with tin shrapnel, and we knew that he was headed for the emergency room again. Worse yet, was his mother ever going to be mad at us now!

Abraham Lincoln once said, "The better part of my life has been my friendships." I feel very lucky for all the friendships that I have had. But Sam? Well, he probably still doesn't feel quite as lucky!

Steady as She Goes

More than half of my patients are on Medicare; thus, I see a lot of elderly people each day. Some are unsteady on their feet, and they wisely use a cane or a walker; however, all too often, I see a patient who had just fallen and is suffering from bruised eyelids, forehead contusions, or broken glasses. My hope is that each of these patients learns from the experience and begins to use a walking aid to prevent future falls. Some people are just too self-conscious or stubborn to do that, however. I am reminded of someone special who fell into that trap and ended up paying a high price.

Alice Mostul and her pastor husband, Hilmar, were great friends of my family for many years. After Hilmar died, Alice chose to live independently in the apartment they'd shared. My wife, Susan, along with others, provided a network of support for her. Alice could still drive her car and had hobbies, friends, and close family members, all of which added to her high quality of life. In public, Alice insisted on dressing smartly and carrying herself well; however, Alice had a long-standing problem with walking. If you watched her walk, you would notice that she often teetered forward and back, as if about to fall over. Her toes were damaged from years of wearing high heels, and her physician felt that she had an inner-ear (balancing) problem, so Alice needed help to walk safely.

A cane and a walker were always available in the apartment, but Alice rarely used either. When we gently mentioned to her one day that using a cane might be safer for her, she would say, "But I'm really doing fine without it today," or "I don't want to take a walker to lunch. What would my friends think?"

On July 3 at about noon, Susie and I stopped in to visit Alice and to remind her that we looked forward to having her over to our Fourth of July celebration. We found her sitting at the kitchen table, still in her nightgown. Remarking that she had fallen in her kitchen the night before, she reassured us that she felt fine. "I know that I should have used my cane, but I didn't," she told us. Susan discovered a large bruise on the back of Alice's head. While I ran out to get Alice a sandwich for lunch, my wife stayed with her and made sure that she was doing okay. We left, fully expecting to see her the next day at our picnic.

Later that same day, however, Alice called our house. Her speech was garbled and we could not understand her. Fearing a stroke, my wife drove over and took her to the hospital emergency room. Alice was admitted to the hospital and spent a few days there. She did well, and there was no evidence of a stroke, so she called and asked us to bring her some fresh clothes and to take her home.

We arrived to find an excited patient happily anticipating a return home. We chatted amicably for a short while, but while helping her prepare to leave, we were alarmed to suddenly hear her again become incoherent and speak in garbled phrases! We wasted no time in calling for help from the staff.

Immediate testing revealed that Alice had suddenly begun to have bleeding in the back of her brain. She was rushed into emergency surgery. Sadly, Alice never regained consciousness and could not be saved. She died two days later.

With good care and a bit of luck, most of us will attain an age when walking accessories will be needed. Remember that falling can cause serious injury! We mustn't let pride or embarrassment stop us from using a cane or walker, for we all need help at some time in our lives. Accepting that help and doing our best is using common sense. To this day, I wish that my dear friend Alice had done as much!

Part Five—Alzheimer's Disease

My father's diagnosis of Alzheimer's disease was completely unexpected. The condition is typically considered an affliction of the elderly. Dad was only sixty-one years old when early mild symptoms began and only sixty-two years old when he was diagnosed. There is another reason my family was caught off guard, however.

My dad's father died from Huntington's disease. This fatal neurologic condition is genetic. My father had a 50 percent chance of inheriting this disease and then dying in his middle age. Five of his brothers and sisters did just that, but Dad had gone to Mayo Clinic when he was fifty-one years old to have Huntington's ruled out. Indeed, he had been told that he had no signs of the disease and that it was likely he had not inherited it.

What a relief that was for our family! Now my brothers, sisters, and I felt free to marry and have children. We stopped worrying that Huntington's was going to kill our father and destroy our futures. In my mind, Dad was one of the lucky ones—but his luck ran out a few years later. In a way, Dad's development of Alzheimer's was an example of poetic injustice. Huntington's destroys the body and leaves the mind still working. Alzheimer's is just the opposite: The body is still healthy while the brain dies. Dad dodged one bullet only to be hit by the other.

These stories represent a sampling of my father's downward spiral but also show that even in my family's darkest hour, there was always hope. You will learn about my mother accepting her role as caregiver and my oldest sister helping us with life-ending decisions, and you will see how I put my father's disease into perspective. The diagnosis of Alzheimer's disease is increasing in frequency. Let's help each other by sharing our experiences.

Caregivers Are Heroes

All of us have probably experienced some important events in our lives that are forever etched into our memories. We can all remember the exact circumstances that we were in when President Kennedy was assassinated or when the space shuttle *Challenger* exploded. Sometimes, such an event can be very personal. It can define how we feel about ourselves or how we feel about another person. Let me take you back to an event that I can remember as if it happened today.

I was sitting in an office with my parents at the Mayo Clinic in Rochester, Minnesota. My sixty-two-year-old father was having mental problems and had just completed two days of extensive medical and psychiatric testing. The neurologist stepped through the door and began to explain to us his diagnosis. He was certain that my dad, despite his age, had developed Alzheimer's disease.

The doctor then spoke to my mother about the course of the disease in a man as young as my dad. He talked about the things that my father would no longer be able to do, and how their lives would have to change. They would need to sell the small gas station that they ran. They would have to sell their trailer house and then move to a town with a nursing home. All of this would need to be done in the near future.

Then the doctor asked my mother if she was experiencing any special difficulties with my dad. I was surprised when my mother replied, "Yes, I am. Every morning for the past forty years, Norb has gotten up first in the morning and he has made the coffee. Now he won't do that anymore. How can I get him to make the coffee again?"

The neurologist put his hand on my mother's shoulder and said softly, "That part of your husband is gone. He'll never be able to make the coffee again." What happened next is what I remember best. Mom looked sadly at my father for a bit, then said, "Well, I'll just have to make that coffee myself. And I guess that I'll have to take care of him too!"

Mom could see her future, and she knew what must be done. She stoically accepted her new role as a care provider. She was now going to help the one person who had helped her most in life. She was still sad about my dad, but she immediately began to stop feeling sad for herself. At that moment, my mother became a hero to me; it is a moment that I remember proudly.

At least once a week in my office, a caregiver will bring in someone for an eye examination. It may be a husband or wife, a grandparent or a neighbor. At the end of the examination, I try to remember to thank that caregiver for bringing the patient in to my office. Occasionally, I look at these caregivers and see my mother again. This memory is a reminder that caregivers are heroes!

Remembering Those Who Can't Remember

Most of us understand that it is the memories of our life experiences that give us our identities. In a very real sense, we are what we remember. Our memories also set us apart from all others as unique individuals, so to lose our memories to something like Alzheimer's disease is to truly lose our individual selves. As sad as this might seem to us, it is good to remember that each of us is part of a family and also part of the community of humanity.

Allow me to tell you about my father to explain what I mean. Dad succumbed to Alzheimer's disease at the age of seventy-one. At the onset of this disease (age sixty-one for Dad), people begin to lose their short-term memories. As time goes on, the pace of loss quickens and the tragedy of the disease reveals itself. Names, dates, faces, events, and all manner of information stored in the brain seem to be lost forever; however, memories that are lost to the victims of Alzheimer's disease are not lost to the rest of us. When we remember these victims, we keep alive their memories for them.

My father, Norbert J. Moritz, the oldest child of eight, was born to poor Kansas wheat farmers. Dad used to tell us stories of the Dust Bowl days. He spoke of clouds of grasshoppers eating the paint from the sides of buildings, of his family setting the table with the plates turned upside down to keep the dust off, and of not having enough food to eat. When my dad was in the eighth grade, his own father died of a fatal neurological disease, so Dad had to quit school, become the head of the family, and run the farm for several years.

His boyhood heroes were the pilots of the barnstormer airplanes, so when the Second World War began, he enlisted and became a pilot. After the war, he went north on a harvesting crew to work in Herrick, South Dakota. Dad stayed there and hired on as a farmhand, eventually marrying the farmer's daughter.

My grandfather let Dad run the farm. We were subsistence farmers, so we butchered our own pigs and rendered our own lard. We milked three cows and raised corn and chickens. For extra money, Dad ran a small gas station and used an Army surplus airplane to crop-dust, but three years of little rain ruined us, so we had to have a farm sale.

The sale was a very sad day in Dad's life, but he did have a plan! We left South Dakota and moved into a one-room apartment in Kansas City (all six of us). There, Dad took a six-week course to learn Morse code and the railroad business. He got a job as a telegrapher on the railroad, pulling us up from poverty into the lower class.

With his steady work, our family grew up happy. Dad loved to fish and bowl. We brewed homemade beer, made ice cream, grew our own vegetables, and canned sauerkraut. It seemed like every meal was potato pancakes, corn on the cob, and a bit of meat from the pressure cooker!

My father never forgot that a little education went a long way. He encouraged his children to go to school. Between us, we five siblings completed twenty-nine years of college. When Dad was fifty-six years old, the railroad went bankrupt and he lost his job. He couldn't find another job, so he and Mom sold their house and returned to South Dakota. There, they bought an old gas station and took up residence in a trailer house behind it. Dad felt at home in that small town, and he loved talking to the farmers when they came to the station for morning coffee and some gas.

This worked well for six good years, up until the day Mom told me that Dad was starting to have some memory problems and that they needed my help. Subsequently, Dad was diagnosed with Alzheimer's disease. We had to sell the gas station and their trailer house when he was sixty-two years old.

It makes me feel very good to remember my father and to know that he enjoyed his family and friends. As I think back, I know that I've learned many important lessons from him: Hard work pays off. When things get tough, just keep going. Take some time to go fishing and embrace the life that you have.

We are half of our mother and half of our father. I like to think that the father half inside me keeps some of my dad alive. His memories are something that I will never forget.

The End of the Line

My father, Norbert J. Moritz, spent much of his working life as an employee of the Rock Island Railroad. He began as a telegrapher and then was a depot agent. Finally, just before the railroad went bankrupt, he worked as a clerk. I can remember him coming home from work one day after twenty-three years on the job and telling me that the company had come to "the end of the line." Six years later, my father would be diagnosed with Alzheimer's disease and thus begin his final journey. Dad died when he was seventy-one years old. Let me tell you what it was like when he got to the end of that line.

End-of-life decisions are not easy. Advanced directives are best thought out ahead of time when we are less emotional and when we have the time to consider our decisions carefully. My older sister, Bobbie, was in charge of my father's health care and his finances. As a registered nurse, she was an ideal person to help the rest of us kids make decisions for Dad. Dr. Dickey was my father's physician, and over the years, he demonstrated genuine care and concern for Dad. There is actually not a lot that a physician needs to do for most patients over much of the course of Alzheimer's disease, but near the end, a caring doctor is very valuable.

Dad's end-of-life decisions were made in two steps, and Dr. Dickey suggested the first step. Dad's disease had advanced to the point that he no longer recognized or remembered any family members and did not comprehend his circumstances. Dr. Dickey suggested that we establish a Do Not Resuscitate order for Dad. This order would mean that if Dad had a stroke or a heart attack, he would not be given extraordinary care. This didn't mean that Dad wouldn't get other health care. When he needed to go to the doctor for injuries, for the flu, or for surgery, he certainly would be cared for properly.

The second step in our end-of-life decision was made after Dad had broken his hip. After the surgery, it was evident that Dad was not cognitively able to benefit from physical therapy and that he could not learn to walk again. He became unaware of his surroundings and could not communicate. Our family had a discussion about what to do if Dad would stop eating. We decided that we should not consider tube feeding to sustain his life. This was a hard decision for us kids to make, but the main burden was left to Bobbie.

During the month of December, Bobbie knew that Dad was having trouble swallowing. One morning, the nursing home called her, explaining that his vital signs were worse and that he had stopped swallowing completely. They were no longer able to feed him. The nurse asked Bobbie if they should order a feeding tube. Relying on our collective decision, Bobbie told the nurse no. Dad was then given pain medication, and he lay quietly in his bed. Four days later, he passed away.

Bobbie would tell you that no one wants to be responsible for someone dying. She had to remind herself that it was the Alzheimer's disease, not the lack of a feeding tube, causing his death. She would also say that a supportive spouse and caring family members are wonderful at a time like that. And her final advice would be that even if your loved one is dying from Alzheimer's and may seem unaware, there is always value in being there for your loved one in his or her final hours.

The end of the line certainly came too soon for my father, but all journeys have a beginning and an end. My father traveled through his life's journey well, and he left a strong family of good people. In some ways, that is the most important thing that each of us can do. The end-of-life decisions that were made for my dad allowed him to die with the dignity that he deserved. My family and I are very thankful that we used advance directives.

The Worst Is First

Some years ago, my father and I were working around his gas station on a hot summer afternoon. We had two jobs to do: dig a long trench in the hard dirt with shovels, and paint the interior of the station. I remember Dad saying, "Let's get the worst over with first, and then the rest won't be so bad," so we grabbed the shovels and got to work!

Dad was diagnosed with Alzheimer's disease when he was sixty-two years old, and he died from it at the age of seventy-one. One of the ironies of Alzheimer's is that the worst comes first. Let me explain what I mean by that.

In the beginning, it was obvious to my family members that something was very wrong with Dad. It wasn't just that he had developed memory problems; he had also stopped working and had lost his appetite. He sat around the house, wouldn't talk to Mom, and looked sad all the time, so we took him to a doctor in Rochester, Minnesota. After careful examination, the neurologist at Mayo Clinic explained his diagnosis of Alzheimer's disease.

The neurologist then suggested that Dad see a psychiatrist at the clinic before we headed back to South Dakota. I was a bit surprised at this suggestion, so the doctor explained that Dad was also exhibiting signs of clinical depression. Now I understood why Dad's behavior had changed so much. Not only was he having memory problems, he also knew that this was happening! He understood more than any of us that his mind was failing and that he was powerless to stop it. Certainly, Dad had a good reason to be depressed!

As his Alzheimer's became worse, my father seemed to accept it better. Of course, now he no longer understood that he was failing. For example, rather than being tormented that he could not recall his children's names, he simply forgot that he had any children! His depression was gone, and we could see that he was more relaxed and in some ways happier than he had been for some time. It was ironic that the worsening disease made my father feel better about himself!

The worst can be first for the friends and relatives of an Alzheimer's patient, too. In the beginning, I saw my father forget the names of his friends and his children. Then, one by one, his recollections of each person disappeared forever. My youngest brother was the first to go, and my oldest sister was the last. I also saw Dad forget how to make change, use his tools, drive a car, and put on his shoes. With each step downward, we knew that we were losing him.

The experience of seeing Dad die mentally was a sad time for all of us, but when it was over, when his mind was gone but his body remained, there was a certain peace for all of us; the hardest part for us, and for him, was over. We weren't waiting for Dad to die anymore. The important part of him was now gone, and we were able to move beyond our grief. We were relieved to know that his suffering was over, and now we could concentrate on seeing that he lived the rest of his time in quiet dignity.

I'm sure that there came a time when my father could no longer recall that hot day when he and I dug the trench together, but I still remember it for him—and I still remember how true his words were when he said, "Let's get the worst over with first, and then the rest won't be so bad."

What Can I Do to Help My Dad?

With the realization that my father had just been given the diagnosis of Alzheimer's disease, I wanted to know how I could help him. This was the first thing that came into my mind when we were in the neurologist's office at Mayo Clinic. A wonderful part of being human is that siblings will often put aside their differences to rally around a stricken parent. This is the way it should be. Being able to help someone who has been told he has a terrible disease makes the bad news easier for us to accept.

Here is some of the advice that the neurologist gave me. First, he said that we should take Dad to a psychiatrist to see if treatment for depression might be in order. Next, we needed to understand that my father should drive a car, operate machinery, and make financial decisions carefully and only with close supervision. The neurologist then said that a general guideline for us would be to try to keep Dad's environment stable, to keep him in a daily routine with his surroundings as stable as possible. Finally, the doctor talked to me about Dad's long-term care needs. For now, he could stay home with my mother, but eventually, he would need to be in a long-term care facility.

We left Mayo Clinic with a heavy hearts but with hope that we could do something positive to make things better, but now my family had a big problem. Mom and Dad lived in a trailer house in a South Dakota town of only seventy people, and none of us kids lived closer than an eight-hour drive! Furthermore, there were no hospitals or nursing homes nearby with facilities for Alzheimer's patients. Finally, Mom had her own serious illness to contend with—advanced emphysema. All of this called for some serious action.

The five of us kids decided to get together and help our parents make some hard decisions. Each of us came in from a different state for a meeting in a hotel room in Iowa. Mom and Dad were there. Everyone brought their own ideas about where our parents should live and how they should be cared for. After a lot of discussion, we reached our decision. The oldest sibling, Bobbie, lived across the street from a good nursing home, and she was a nurse. Plus, she was a nursing home inspector, so she knew a lot about Alzheimer care units. We agreed to have Mom and Dad move to her town and live there until Dad needed nursing home care. The rest of us kids would visit, and we would send money to Bobbie each month to help with extra expenses.

My mother liked this plan except for one thing. She turned to me and said, "Bert, the doctor at Mayo Clinic said that we should keep everything the same for Norb. It'll be hard on him if we move him, so maybe we shouldn't go anywhere." I understood Mom's fear. After all, my sister lived in Boise, Idaho, and that's a long way from South Dakota! So what was our solution to help Mom feel better and to keep Dad's environment as stable as possible? The rest of us decided that we'd move their trailer house to Boise and have it ready when they got there. And that, my friends, is exactly what we did! When Dad got out of my car, he walked right into the trailer house, thinking he was still in South Dakota. He settled right in and never seemed at all concerned.

Meeting the short-term and long-term needs of a seriously ill person is not easy, but with the good advice of a doctor and with the help of friends and family, we can make the best of a difficult situation. For us, moving a house to Idaho was not easy, but having the peace of mind that we had helped our dad was well worth it!

What Don't They Know?

My father was diagnosed with Alzheimer's disease at age sixty-two. He and my mother continued to live in their trailer house in South Dakota for four years after his diagnosis. They ran a small gas station, and Dad would occasionally drive a tractor for one of his farmer friends. During those years, each of us five kids took turns spending long weekends at their place, helping Mom and working around the business.

During the time I spent with my father, I noticed that his mind was slowly changing. It became hard to know what things Dad could do and what things he had forgotten. For example, was he still safe driving a car, or was it time to take the keys away? It's really hard to know what someone else doesn't know! Let me give you a few examples.

The first time I suspected that my father was failing happened while we were working on a car at the station. As had been the case since my boyhood, Dad did all the work and I was reduced to handing him the tools and being the go-fer! Near the end of the job this day, he called for a screwdriver. I handed it to him, and he gingerly held it up to the screw. He abruptly stopped and remained motionless for a few seconds. Then he turned and said to me, "I know this sounds funny, but I can't remember how to use this tool." Amazed and disturbed by his admission, I then helped him finish the job. Little did I know that my father would never again use a screwdriver.

People with Alzheimer's can be very crafty at hiding their inabilities. On the day we were moving Mom and Dad out of the trailer house, one of Dad's longtime friends, named Walt, approached us. Walt began by telling me that we were making a mistake in moving Dad away for professional care. As far as Walt could tell, there was nothing wrong with Dad. He went on to relate that Dad had recently helped him on the farm and that Dad had done just fine. I turned to Dad and, referring to Walt, asked him, "Who is this man?"

Dad replied, "He is a very fine man, and I'm glad to meet him." I then asked Dad what the man's name was, and Dad replied, "Well, I'm not sure, but I know that he is a fine man." Walt was stunned that Dad didn't even know him anymore! With this, Walt sadly came to understand that it was time for my father to leave.

A final example I want to share with you illustrates that even in the darkest of times, humor or even a touch of pleasure can be found in caring for someone with Alzheimer's disease.

Shortly after my mother's death, I had the job of getting Dad dressed for her funeral. He and I were in his nursing home room, and I had just slipped a shoe on one of his feet, but getting the other one on turned into a struggle. I pushed and pushed, but no matter how hard I tried, I just couldn't get his foot in! Meanwhile, Dad kept saying to me, "There's something in there." I just assumed he was confused, so I continued to try all the harder.

Finally, I stopped and just sat there on the floor in front of him. I glanced up at Dad, and he said, "There's something in there," so I turned the shoe over, and sure enough, a metal shoehorn tumbled to the floor. When I looked back up, Dad smiled broadly at me and said, "See!" We both had a hard laugh together on that one! So, indeed, it is hard to know what they don't know, and it's equally hard to know what they do know!

Why Me?

As an eye doctor, I see a wide range of patient responses to health problems. Most patients understand that the long road of life is full of bumps and potholes; they don't like bad news, but they often overcome their problems and then go on to live productive, happy lives. When a relative or spouse becomes ill, however, it is difficult to predict how each of us will respond to their disease. We can give them some support, but for the most part, we are helpless to change their fates.

Let me tell you about how I was once affected by a disease that someone close to me had developed. My father was fifty-six years old when the railroad he worked for went bankrupt. Dad couldn't find a job in that industry, so he and Mom sold their Iowa house and moved back to South Dakota. They bought an old gas station with a trailer house out back. For five years, they were content to pump gas, sell groceries, and socialize with old friends. Then, Dad got sick.

His illness came on gradually. Mom would mention that he seemed to lose his way while driving out in the country, or that he would forget to do some routine work around the station. When I visited them, I noticed that Dad had trouble using simple tools when he was repairing engines. Also, he kept asking me, "Which way is north?" He had been a pilot in the Army Air Corps and had always prided himself on knowing his directions. At this point, none of this bothered me very much, for he was getting a bit older and maybe some of this was normal.

Then Dad got much worse! He became so confused that he couldn't do his job. One day, he got lost and ended up in Nebraska! Finally, he became clinically depressed, so I took him to Mayo Clinic in Rochester. When the doctor turned to me and said that Dad had Alzheimer's disease, it felt like a punch to the gut! I might have suspected this all along, but I sure did not want to hear it. Not my dad ... not my family ... not me!

The long drive back was really hard for me. I wasn't just stunned and sad but felt like the world was closing in on me. There were so many questions running in my mind about my parents' future that I was confused and couldn't concentrate on any single issue. The whole world seemed dark and small, as if the future did not extend beyond the hood of the car!

When I got back to Wisconsin, I went to my office. I wasn't looking forward to seeing my patients as I usually did. The work-days seemed to last forever, and it was hard to think of anything besides my father. I talked to friends about Dad's disease, and they said that they felt sorry for me, so I began to feel sorry for myself and started to think that I was sick! After a bit of reflection, I soon realized that depression was setting in and that something was wrong with my thinking. Clearly, it was time to do better!

First, I talked to my doctor about my feelings. He suggested that I read a book about Alzheimer's so I would better understand the disease. This gave me a good start. Then my wife said that I needed to be more involved in my parents' lives and that I should help them prepare for the future, so I began driving back and forth from Wisconsin to South Dakota over a series of long weekends. This really helped me! I worked with Mom to set up their finances and took Dad out to buy a new car. Dad couldn't drive it, but he enjoyed looking at the cars and trying them on for size! Together with my siblings, I got their trailer house ready to move and the gas station ready to sell.

Learning about Alzheimer's disease and helping my parents prepare for their future was terrific therapy for me! I stopped feeling sorry for myself, and I stopped feeling like I was sick! We have to be careful that we don't develop a "Why me?" attitude when confronted with a sick friend or relative. We instead need to concentrate on positive actions that will help them through their illness and that will help us cope with our own feelings. We owe it to ourselves and to our loved ones.

Part Six—Army Days

When I was drafted into the United States Army, I was nineteen years old. I had just finished my first year of college with mediocre grades and no career path in mind. Talk about wet behind the ears! I saw more of life during my two years of service than I had ever dreamed existed. My basic-training platoon included African Americans, Native Americans, Mexican Americans, Asian Americans, and just plain old Americans. In those days, you had to be twenty-one years old to drink alcohol, and the Army had just introduced their "beer in the barracks" experiment. Let me tell you, that idea didn't last very long!

This was not an ideal time to be inducted into military service. (Is there ever an ideal time?) The war in Vietnam was winding down, and it wasn't going well for our side. Morale was low, and the military needed to change. Despite these issues, my experience was very positive. I matured in the military, and the GI Bill was my ticket to higher education and a better life.

I served fifteen months in a combat zone along the Demilitarized Zone between North and South Korea. I did not serve in Vietnam. My stories are not about valor and war heroes. Instead, you will read about leaving my family, training, eating Army food, and doing a job. When I think back on my Army days, I remember only the good times. If you have served, you might identify with my experiences. If you have not served, then I hope these stories will give you a glimpse into a part of our society that has a culture like no other.

I Got By with a Little Help

When I was a boy, one of my jobs was to polish my father's good shoes. I usually did this chore Saturday night so they were shined up for Sunday Mass. I noticed that Dad's shoes had holes in the soles, and I remember thinking that the old guy was just too cheap to buy a new pair. Once I got a bit older and a lot wiser, I realized that Dad hadn't bought new shoes for a good reason. With his eighth-grade education and job as a railroad telegrapher, there just wasn't enough money to go around. He sacrificed himself to help the family. I think we can all remember some special things that our parents did that helped us while we were growing up. Here are a few of the things that my parents did for me.

My brothers, sisters, and I all had one thing in common. We all were very near sighted, and we needed new eyeglass lenses every year. Mom would march me down to the optometrist's office before school started, and I would have to answer the question "Which is better, one or two?" I usually had to keep the same black frames, and then Dad would get a bill for only the new lenses. I could then see the school's blackboard again. Little did my parents know that by sending me to the optometrist, they not only helped me in school but also influenced my eventual career choice!

My father gave me lots of advice, not the least of which included how to buy life insurance, how to tie a necktie, and how to catch and clean a walleye. He was as generous with gifts as his income allowed, and there were two items Dad gave me that I have never forgotten.

The night before I left for the Army, Dad did something that he had never done before—he invited me out for a beer. After he drove me to the Hilltop Supper Club at the edge of town, we sat down at the bar and he ordered each of us an Andeker beer. Now, I had never heard of this beer before, so Dad explained that it was a premium brew made by Pabst Blue Ribbon and that this was a drink for special occasions. The bartender brought the beers in a special pair of tall Andeker glasses. When we had finished, Dad paid for the beer, and he bought those glasses too. On the way home, he told me that he would add them to his beer-glass collection. Then he went on to explain that when I came home from the service, those two glasses would be mine. I realized at that moment that Dad was worried I might not come back and this was his way of letting me know that I would be on his mind. I remember feeling good that Dad would be thinking of me, but I was also a bit frightened.

A year later when I was stationed overseas, I was pleasantly surprised to receive a letter from Dad. As it turned out, that was the only letter my father would ever write to me! At the end of the letter, he reminded me that those two beer glasses were still in his cabinet and that I could have them upon my return.

Sadly, I ended up losing that letter, and to this day, I wish I could read it and see my father's handwriting again. Fortunately, though, those two Andeker glasses now reside in my living room cabinet, along with the rest of Dad's collection. Each time I look at them, I see the special things that my parents did to help me get by when I was growing up.

Fickle

I took my Army basic training at Fort Leonard Wood in Missouri. On the first day there, uniforms were issued. After waiting in a long line to be measured for boots and clothes, I had a bunch of shirts, pants, and underwear thrown in my direction. I scooped the stuff up and jammed it all in a duffle bag. Back at the barracks, my civilian clothes were mailed home and I put on my new fatigues.

For a nineteen-year-old, I was pretty scrawny; I weighed just 118 pounds. I didn't need a mirror to know that my new Army duds were way too big! I immediately marched outside and walked right up to the drill sergeant. "Sergeant," I said, "my clothes don't fit! They are the wrong size." Senior Drill Sergeant Potts (who eventually turned out to be the loudest, meanest sergeant I would ever encounter) looked at the name on my shirt. "Who do you think I am, Private Moritz," he bellowed, "your mommy? The Army has two sizes: two too big and two too small! Now get down and give me fifty push-ups, soldier! And then get your baggy self out of my sight!"

As I go through life, I try to draw on words of wisdom that have been offered to me along the way. One day, while examining a farmer, I sat and listened to him express concern about the weather. He said that the spring had been too cool and too wet and that the summer was too hot and too dry. This brought back those fateful words from my drill sergeant, "two too big and two too small." I then realized that the sergeant had been telling me that there will be always something to complain about but often little that can be done about it!

The weather is a prime example. Here are a few examples detailing how weather extremes have affected my life:

Too much snow. Up to the day I was born, December 18, 1952, South Dakota had been very dry. On that day, my father was so nervous after my birth that he forgot to release the parking brake on his pickup. As he drove home, sparks flew from under the truck and started our cornfield on fire! Then it began to snow! It snowed so much that the storm was named the Blizzard of the Rosebud (we lived near the Rosebud Indian Reservation). My older sister spent three days trapped in the school. Entire houses were covered under drifts, several people died, and thousands of beef cattle suffocated. This was an early warning that weather and I were not going to get along!

Too much cold. Some years later when I was a boy, we lived in Estherville, Iowa. I operated two paper routes: a morning route and an evening route. Estherville is known for two things: a big meteor that had fallen there, and the invention of the word *blizzard* by the local newspaper editor! Believe me, your paperboy knows what that word means: a huge snowstorm followed by high winds and subzero temperatures. At the time, those storms weren't uncommon, so town folk expected newspaper delivery regardless. Walking in that cold, I'd end up with frozen feet! After my paper deliveries, Mom would fill a pan with cold water and I'd soak my painful feet to let them warm up slowly!

Too dry. A poorly timed drought redirected the course of my life many years ago. My family started out living in the back of a gas station, but Dad was a farmer at heart, so he took over a farm near Herrick, South Dakota. It didn't go very well because there was no rain the following three summers. Thus, we lost the farm and had to move on. I wonder today, Would I be a farmer had the weather not intervened?

Too much wind. My age of innocence came to an end when a tornado destroyed the house over our heads outside of Vinton, Iowa. That was the day that my older sister told me there was no Santa Claus! Excessive winds also helped me decide against a career in the US Army. When a typhoon hit the Demilitarized Zone in Korea, our captain ordered us to throw sandbags on the equipment to keep it from blowing away. Every time I dropped a sandbag, I was in danger of being blown off the mountaintop myself! High winds even tried to keep me from living in Eau Claire, Wisconsin. While traveling to Minneapolis in July of 1980, my wife and I decided to spend the night resting in an Eau Claire hotel. Unfortunately, a straight-line windstorm swept through town with winds in excess of one hundred miles per hour! The roof of our hotel blew off while my wife and I huddled in the bathtub! When we left Eau Claire next morning, I promised that we would never come back!

We all have to accept that there will always be some factors in our lives we can't control. Recall how I wasn't aware of this maxim as a young soldier in my unwillingness to accept those jumbo-sized uniforms. As soon as I could, I hired a Korean tailor to alter those uniforms for a better fit. Thus, when I was discharged from the Army, I left in a crisp, well-fitting dress uniform. Well, I found that uniform in the basement the other day. I tried it on ... and discovered that it was now two sizes too small!

Forced March

I was drafted during the Vietnam War. My basic training was at Fort Leonard Wood in Missouri. The Army used that training time to teach us important lessons of discipline and esprit de corps. It was also necessary to make each of us physically fit in the event we ended up in combat. They took this very seriously! We had to do fifty sit-ups, fifty push-ups, and twenty pull-ups before each meal. Every morning, we did two miles of the "airborne shuffle." Sometimes we also ran again in the evening. At the beginning of our training, the drill sergeants warned us that our most difficult day would be when we were made to do a forced march of seven miles. I dreaded that day.

It was a typical cool November day. We had finished morning chow, and our company formed up for the day's activities. Picture 200 soldiers dressed in Army-green combat fatigues and wearing black boots, steel helmets, and full backpacks, each holding an M-16 rifle. We stood in rows of twelve—four platoons of forty-eight men each. I was the first squad leader of the first platoon, so my position was at the very front corner. The expectation was that Senior Drill Sergeant Potts would take us on our morning run, followed by training. Instead, and much to our surprise, three jeep ambulances pulled up behind the formation.

I then spied a soldier marching confidently toward the front of the formation. I had never seen anyone like him before! He was an African American who must have stood all of 6'4", weighed 230 pounds (solid muscle), and wore an officer's uniform. I could see that he had a silver eagle on his collar, a rifle and a parachute patch sewn on his chest, and a shoulder patch depicting a pine tree. Thus, he was a full-bird colonel who had carried a rifle in Vietnam, qualified as a paratrooper, and was a member of the Special Forces as a Green Beret! I didn't know what was about to happen, but I knew that it wasn't going to be good!

The colonel called us to attention. Four hundred boots snapped together. "Men," he shouted, "this morning you will complete your required forced march of seven miles." And then in a command voice, he barked, "Left *face!*" And there I stood at the very top of the column as the colonel positioned himself right beside me! I was shaking in my boots when he looked down at me and said, "Soldier, you *will* keep up with me, stride for stride. Is that understood?"

Looking up at the massive warrior, I opened my mouth and squeaked out a feeble "Yes, sir."

Seven hard miles later, we came to a stop at exactly the same spot from where we started. The colonel barked, "Right *face!*" And there we stood, trying to keep at attention, uniforms soaked in sweat, most guys doubled over, and breathing so hard that we were shaking. Three soldiers in my platoon had fallen out and had to be picked up by the ambulances. One from my squad had broken his ankle. "I want you men to know that it was an honor to serve with you this morning!" the colonel said. Then, as he saluted the company, he continued, "This has been the most homogenous unit that I have ever marched with. *Dismissed!*"

As that impressive soldier spoke those words, I noticed that the men in the first platoon straightened up and stood tall. The Army's ideals of discipline and esprit de corps were apparent to us at that moment. The company, each platoon, each squad, and each individual had learned much more than what we could do; we had learned what we could do together!

Hot Rats

Raised in small South Dakota and Iowa towns, I certainly wasn't very worldly. We couldn't afford a fancy vacation, so a big trip for us was a hot July ride in Dad's old station wagon to visit Grandma. When it was time to go Christmas shopping, we drove over to the big town of Gregory—population 1,143! Of course, I thought that I was a man about town and that I was ready for anything. Then I got drafted and sent to the Army! You don't need to take a class in sociology to learn about human nature when you are living with a hundred men in a small barracks. Talk about an eye opener! And the lessons I learned...

After completing basic training in Missouri, I was sent to Fort Bliss, Texas, for missile training. This was right across the border from Juarez, Mexico. Talk about hot, dusty sandstorms!

The only redeeming quality of that duty station was the food. Boy, could those Army cooks make a great meal! Good food is very important to a lonely soldier far from home.

When my training was done, I got orders to go overseas to South Korea. I was assigned to a combat zone, on a mountaintop overlooking the Demilitarized Zone, for more than a year. But at least the food would be good—right?

Nope. The food was terrible: powdered eggs, powdered milk, powdered mashed potatoes—and that was just for breakfast! I couldn't believe it. Our mess sergeant would ruin a piece of toast! At least two nights a week, up on the mountain, he would serve us some kind of meat that we never could recognize. We came to call it "hot rats." Oddly, the mess sergeant never came to appreciate our humor!

One boring day, I was sitting with some of my buddies on a wall of sandbags surrounding the mess hall. Derrick, a tall red-headed kid from Kentucky, spied a dead rat lying nearby. "It must have eaten last night's leftovers," he speculated, "because I still feel a bit sick, myself." Someone asked Derrick what he was going to do with the rat. After a bit of consideration (Derrick wasn't a real quick thinker), he got an idea. "We'll give Cookie some help with tonight's meal. Let's heat it up and then sneak into the kitchen!"

Now, I'd like to say that I wasn't too involved in this caper. I was the technical specialist of the bunch, however, so I suggested that we use one of the radars. I explained to the guys that one of our radars had a high gain antenna horn and that it emitted microwaves. This was before microwave ovens were invented, but I figured that if it could track a MIG 23 jet from fifty miles away, it ought to be able to cook a rat!

One guy found a long pole and some string. We tied one end onto the dead rat's tail and the other end to the pole. I lowered the antenna in altitude until it pointed toward the ground. Then, being careful not to get in front of the antenna, we hung that expired critter about six inches from the transmitter horn. It wasn't long before there was abundant smoke! Three of us, the brave ones, then put the hot meal in a paper bag for delivery to the cook.

We found Cookie behind the mess hall, having a smoke. In making our presentation, we told him, "Here's another hot rat that you can add to tonight's dinner menu." We almost busted a gut laughing, but he didn't crack a smile. After looking into the bag, he summarily grabbed the tail and tossed our little buddy down the mountain!

Well, that ill-tempered mess sergeant's rotation was over in March. The day after he left, a new cook took over. Our first breakfast was bacon and real eggs, waffles with syrup, and fresh cornbread! And I'll never forget that first night's dinner: steak and shrimp, baked potato, and a trailer loaded with ice-cold beer. We just couldn't believe it! What had happened, and why the good food now? It didn't take us long to realize that the old cook had been selling our good food in the village below and serving us spare Army battle rations! Derrick suggested that if we ever caught the guy, we should hang him in front of that radar. We all agreed in unison!

When we are young, we think we know everything. My stint in the Army taught me a lot about the world and about people. When I got out, I still didn't know everything, but at least I knew a lot more than when I went in!

Three, Two, One —We Have Lift-off!

When I was a boy, I had a couple of paper routes. I'd get up early in the morning and lug a bundle of *Des Moines Register* newspapers on the back of my bicycle through the neighborhoods. After school, I'd take around the *Des Moines Tribune*. This was real work for a kid, especially in the winter. My motivation? Pure and simple: money for rockets!

My brother and I would buy solid-fuel rocket engines through the mail. Then we would build our rockets from kits or we would design them ourselves. We seemed to always take our hobbies to their logical extreme, and rocketry was no exception! Our rockets got bigger and bigger until we stuffed multiple long-range engines into Big Bertha. Finally, we couldn't make them any bigger, so for added fun, we decided to make them explode! Dave, my older teen brother, concocted an explosive powder out of mail-order chemicals. We then packed charges onto the top of our launch vehicles. Today, we'd likely be investigated for suspected terrorism, but back then, we were just a couple of inventive kids having fun.

A few years passed, and before I knew it, I was being drafted into the United States Army and sent to Missouri for basic training. At the end of basic, I was standing in line with the other guys in my company when orders were passed out. Imagine my surprise when I read my orders—I was being sent to Texas for training as a Hawk fire control missile crewman. My job was going to be to shoot rockets—really big rockets!

After the training in Texas, the Army shipped me off for duty to the Demilitarized Zone between North and South Korea. My unit was assigned to the top of a mountain, and it had the distinction of being the highest Army tactical site in the world! Our battery consisted of six launchers, each fitted with three rockets. Each rocket was about as long as a kitchen and about as wide as a fifty-five-gallon drum. I was the tactical command assistant for the unit, and my duties included identifying enemy targets and firing the missiles. As such, I spent much of my time in a small electronics van that held five men.

Our job was to launch Hawk surface-to-air rockets at incoming enemy aircraft in the event of war. This was quite challenging and not easily done, given the lack of simulator technology at the time; thus, we needed live-fire practice. So in August, my unit was sent down to a firing range along the coast of the Yellow Sea near Incheon, Korea.

The range was right on the beach, and I could see our Hawk missiles facing the water, ready for firing. To my surprise, a much larger rocket was waiting on its launch platform behind the Hawks! It was a black and white multistage Nike Hercules missile standing straight up. Our captain announced that the Nike would be going up first and that we would follow. Further, he informed us that a group of US senators, along with some American and Korean generals, were here to observe us.

My crew was then herded into a long trench that left our heads just above the ground. A very thick piece of Plexiglas stood between the launchers and us. We were told that the Nike missile was going to gain altitude, turn left, and then explode out over the ocean. We heard the countdown begin! I had my camera pointed at the launch pad and could see smoke coming out the bottom of the rocket. And then, in the blink of an eye and with a burst of flames, it was gone, straight up, and so fast that I couldn't believe it!

Craning our necks, we could see just a small glowing speck above us—but it did not turn left out to sea! Instead, it turned right, heading inland! At that moment, some officer must have realized that the missile was out of control, so he hit the DESTROY button. We then saw a small burst of light and then heard a muffled explosion. Moments later, rocket fragments began to fall to Earth, heading right toward us! Remember the trench we were in? It had no roof, and the protective Plexiglas would do us no good! Huge chucks of twisted metal splashed into the ocean and hit the firing base all around us. Luckily, no one was hurt.

And then it was our turn. I had a feeling that the senators and generals were not impressed so far. As my crew scrambled to the Hawk equipment, a radio-controlled jet drone was being launched. Once in the air, it was to release a reflective target that it towed on a long line. Our job would be to shoot down the target while avoiding the expensive drone.

I assumed my duty station before the radar screen in the van with our unit commander, a captain, at my side. We could see only one blip moving on the radar screen, and I knew that it signified the drone. Apparently, the towed target had not deployed properly, so we waited patiently for it to do so.

We continued to track the drone for about twenty minutes. Suddenly, the van door flew open and in burst some red-faced and very angry general. "What's going on? Why haven't you fired?" he shouted.

The captain stammered, "We can't find the target, sir."

The general's response was blunt: "I want something shot out of the sky, and I want it shot down *now*! Do you hear me, soldier?"

He was looking in my direction when he yelled that. I barked, "Lock on the drone!" and then "Fire!" The van shook as a Hawk missile exploded off the launcher and streaked skyward! The captain and I watched as the drone's radar blip blinked off the screen, knowing that a lot of taxpayer dollars had just fallen into the salt water!

I still love rockets. As a child, playing with them was a way to escape the boredom of small-town life. As a soldier, they were a means to do my duty for my country. And now whenever I see a rocket launched, I am reminded of the fun that I had, and of the optimism that I still have for the future!

Senior Drill Sergeant Potts

I was drafted into the United States Army during the Vietnam War. After my medical physical, I was sent to Fort Leonard Wood, in Missouri, for basic training. What an experience that was! There were literally thousands of young men being indoctrinated into the Army way of life and, at the same time, being whipped into good physical shape.

This was a tough time to be in the Army. Some of us would be headed for combat, so having a strong body and knowing how to shoot accurately was very important. The tough job of getting that done was given to the army DIs (drill instructors). Our DIs were the toughest, meanest sons of guns that this young guy had ever come across, but they had served in the war, and they had our long-term best interest at heart.

Let me tell you a bit about our senior drill sergeant. His name was Potts, and he was 5'1", strong as a bull, and tough as nails. He had a couple of Bronze Stars on his office wall from his service in Vietnam. Potts had no tolerance for recruits expressing opinions to him, and we were likely to do fifty push-ups every time we came close to annoying him. When we would do especially painful group exercises, he would scream, "What's the good word?!" and the entire company would yell back, "Endurance, endurance!" When he barked, "Jump!" all we asked was "How high, Senior Drill Sergeant?"

I distinctly recall the first time we met Senior Drill Sergeant Potts. He had called the platoon together on the third day of basic training for an announcement. At the top of his voice, he shouted, "First platoon has a problem. First platoon has a big problem. Robertson is overweight. Now, until Robertson makes weight, this platoon will run two extra miles each night and do one hundred extra sit-ups and fifty extra push-ups before each meal!" At that point, thirty-nine men turned and glared at Robertson. What we saw was an eighteen-year-old pimple-faced kid who looked like a fat Jackie Gleason! He had the shape of a bowling pin, and we were all going to get punished for it!

So how did we handle it? It took us just a couple of days to realize that Robertson was not likely to sweat his way to thinness very quickly, so we decided it was time for him to go on a diet! We reasoned that the more food we kept from him, the smaller he would get and the sooner we could stop the extra workouts, so each time Robertson went through the chow line, we took food off of his tray.

One day during training, our platoon headed out to the grenade range. In this exercise, we learned to throw a live hand grenade safely. Doing it safely is not as easy as it sounds. It's fair to say that no one can throw a grenade far enough away to keep it from killing the thrower, so you need to be behind something before it blows up!

All forty of us were ordered into a long trench that had a Plexiglas shield around it. This way, we would be safely below ground level yet could get our heads just above ground to watch the exercise. One by one, we'd be called out of the trench and told to run forward to a foxhole. Once there, we were to jump in and throw a live grenade. In the foxhole with us would be Senior Drill Sergeant Potts. He would hand the soldier a grenade and watch as the soldier armed the grenade and then threw it downrange. When the grenade exploded, we were expected to hug the bottom of that foxhole for all we were worth!

The whole exercise was going pretty well. We each took our turn until we were down to the last one in the platoon … Robertson. Still way overweight, with his uniform just starting to hang loose, he plodded out to the foxhole and plopped down in it. We could see that the kid was terrified and shaking hard! Potts then handed him the grenade. Robertson managed to pull the pin, and then he popped off the arming handle. So what did he do next? He just dropped that live grenade, right in the foxhole with them both!

For those of us watching, it was like time had suddenly stopped. We were stunned, and we all watched in horror, expecting an explosion! Suddenly, the senior drill sergeant's right hand shot forward and grasped Robertson's neck. At the same time, with his left hand, he grabbed Robertson's belt. Then, what had to be the shortest DI in the US Army lifted the fattest guy in our company right up out of that foxhole and threw him to safety! Next, Potts executed a quick roll backward out of the foxhole. The grenade blew up. Now, I would like to say that the DI and Robertson shared a big, tearful hug after that one, but to be honest, let's just say that Senior Drill Sergeant Potts came off the ground in a very foul mood and directed some pointed words at Robertson!

By the end of basic training, the initial fear we'd all had for our senior drill sergeant was replaced by deep respect. Each of us was then assigned to an advanced training station, except Robertson. And what became of him? Well, despite our rationing of his food and the platoon's extra calisthenics, he never made weight. He even had to rely on a rope to hold up his loose trousers, but he was still too heavy, so he had to go back through basic training again, and I would guess that some other new platoon had a big problem!

Part Seven—Stories from the Office

Most of us can remember our career-dilemma days. When we were young, we asked ourselves, "What am I going to be when I grow up?" When we were grown up, some of us still had no idea, so I can empathize with young people who ask me how I chose to become an optometrist. They are floundering and seeking a way out of their dilemma, so here is what I tell them.

I did not become an eye doctor to save people from blindness. There was no magic moment when I had a mystical calling to do good or to help humanity. In fact, I didn't actively choose to become a doctor at all. You see, I actually wanted to *become my eye doctor*. I didn't want his occupation—I wanted to be him.

My optometrist was Dr. Jim Roberts. He had a wife and two children. They dressed well, and they lived in a house that was nicer than ours. Dr. Roberts was well-spoken and respected in our community, and he seemed to enjoy life. He would reduce his fees to our family on the cost of eyeglasses. Above all, he treated me kindly when not many other adults did. I wanted to become the person that Dr. Roberts was.

So, in advising young people, I say, "Don't go to college to get a job. Go to college to become a better person. Think of someone you admire, and strive to be like her or him. Learn to speak well, to make good judgments, to understand the world you live in. What you learn in college is not nearly as important as the kind of person you become. Be a good person and you will excel at any career that follows."

My office stories are fun. I have examined more than 150,000 patients (nearly 300,000 eyes), so there have been plenty of opportunities for human interaction. Among others, you are going to read about a Chicago cop and a Baptist minister. Each became one of many memories I have from my practice.

The Best-Laid Plans

Years ago, after a busy day in the clinic, I wanted to get home and do some odd jobs around the house. While driving home from work, I was in car accident.

Traffic was heavy but moving along briskly on Eau Claire's main thoroughfare. Up ahead, the traffic light switched to red. Everyone braked, and we came to a complete stop. The vehicle directly ahead of me was a large SUV with a big trailer hitch. I'd stopped about ten feet behind it and was sitting quietly, waiting for the light to turn green. Then with no warning whatsoever, I was stunned to see the SUV ahead of me traveling backward! That crazy driver was going to hit me, so I braced myself for impact as the SUV accelerated toward me! At the instant of impact, I was once again stunned, but not by the force! I was suddenly struck by the realization that the SUV wasn't moving back toward me—it was my car rolling forward, and I had just hit the SUV! I sure was embarrassed as I apologized to the other driver. To this day, I have no idea why I absentmindedly drove into the back of that vehicle.

Sometimes, events just don't go the way I expect. You might think that after thirty-five years of practice and seeing tens of thousands of patients, I would have this eye-examination routine down pat, but there have been times when I have had to apologize to my patients. More often than not, the recipients of my apologies tend to be female! Let me give you a few examples of how a simple eye examination can go awry in my office.

A pleasant, middle-aged woman came to the office, claiming that something was stuck in her right eye. This was fairly unusual, for most patients with this complaint tend to be male. (Imagine lying on the ground under a vehicle while pounding on a rusty muffler without wearing safety glasses.) This lady complained of something under her upper eyelid, however; thus, I needed to turn the eyelid over and inspect the underside with my microscope. While staring intently into the microscope, I grasped her eyelashes and pulled up while simultaneously thrusting the back of the lid downward. Imagine my surprise when the lid remained stationary and I witnessed all of her eyelashes tearing off! Leaning back, I could see that I was holding her artificial eyelashes between my fingers. Oops! Time for an apology!

Early in my career, I worked as a one-man operation, performing many specialty tests by myself. One day, an elderly woman needed a visual-field test to rule out glaucoma. I placed a black "pirate's patch" over her left eye and proceeded to test the right eye. When done with the first eye, I needed to remove the patch and place it over the other eye. While she was facing me, I grasped the patch and slid it up and back over her head. I must have had it on a bit tight, because it hooked on her hair. To my horror, I knocked her hair off right onto the floor! I certainly hadn't expected a wig, and I definitely won't forget the look on that poor woman's face. She'll remember the egg on my face, too!

As you might expect, understanding fashion in women's clothing is not my forte. Well, twenty-five years ago, I was looking into the eyes of a pleasant and well-dressed eighty-four-year-old woman. Noticing retinal changes that suggested problems with hypertension, I asked her to remove her jacket so I could check the blood pressure in her left arm. I turned away on my chair and found my blood pressure cuff in a desk drawer. Swiveling back toward her, I was stunned to see her sitting in the examination chair, dressed from the waist up in only a bra—and a leopard-print one, at that! I don't remember if she had problems with her blood pressure, but I know I was pretty red-faced at that moment!

By now, you may have reached the conclusion that whenever something goes wrong in my office, I am generally at fault. This is mostly true, but this last example is a bit more complicated than that. I had started practicing at a large medical clinic in Minneapolis in 1980, and it was my second day on the job. A striking woman of Asian descent had come in for an examination. She was dressed in a beautiful pink dress and seemed quite well educated. After I took her case history, we had a short conversation.

"Do you know who I am?" she asked.

Glancing down at the chart, I could see her name, but I didn't recognize it. "No, I am not familiar with you, ma'am."

She told me her name, then said, "I wrote a chapter for the Betty Crocker cookbook. I have a restaurant here in Minneapolis. You should come and enjoy a dinner at my restaurant. The food is excellent."

I asked her the name of the restaurant and thanked her.

The rest of the eye examination proceeded without incident until the last test. I needed to check her eye pressure to rule out the disease glaucoma. To perform that test, I had to put an eye drop in each eye. As I was bringing the eyedropper near her face, I inadvertently squeezed it and a single drop fell onto the shoulder of her dress. I was horrified! That yellow fluorescein dye stood out like a bull in a china shop! Knowing that honesty is the best policy, I swallowed my pride and pointed out my error. I don't think she actually heard my apology, for she was overcome with anger! She went on about how expensive the dress was and asking what I was going to do about it. Two weeks later, the clinic administration sent me her bill for a new dress. I paid it, but to this day, I have never eaten at her restaurant!

The great American author John Steinbeck once wrote, "The best laid plans of mice and men often go awry." There are many bumps on the road of life, and along the way, there are going to be some problems with our plans. I understand all that. I just wish I could steer my car of life a little better so I could avoid some of those self-inflicted potholes!

Career Choice

One of the great pleasures I have experienced in my career is talking to young people who are to going on to college. I enjoy asking them about their career goals and their choices of college major. Every once in a while, a young person asks me how I decided to became an eye doctor. Here is what I tell them.

My parents were not highly educated; in fact, my dad did not go beyond the eighth grade in school, so just having the opportunity to go to college was a big deal for me. When I started college, I had no idea whatsoever I wanted to have a career in.

Becoming an optometrist was never on my mind, so for my first year of college, I took the usual classes in English, speech, chemistry, and mathematics. My grades were OK, but I was still an uninspired student who wasn't sure what to do next. When the summer came around, I took a job working on the railroad. Then one day that summer, President Nixon sent me a letter. Even before opening it, I knew exactly what I was going to be—I was going to be a soldier. I had just been drafted into the Army.

A year and a half later, I came home from overseas on what the Army called rest and relaxation. My friends were all working or away at college, which left me little to do around town. I used to fly gas-powered model airplanes, so I decided to work on the old planes that were still in the basement of my parents' house. I remember hearing that my optometrist, Dr. Jim Roberts, had flown model planes, too, so I decided to visit him to see what he had been building.

Dr. Roberts was someone I admired. He was young and hardworking, and he cared about my family members when we were in his office. All five of us kids and my parents needed eyeglasses, so we were in his office a lot! Dad spoke highly of him, and I knew that he had reduced the bill to our family on many an occasion.

I was a bit nervous when I rang Dr. Roberts's doorbell. I had never been to his house and wondered how he would react to me. He was well-dressed, articulate, self-assured, and very nice to me. Dr. Roberts invited me downstairs, and we spent an hour or two talking about his airplanes. As we came back upstairs, he shook my hand, I thanked him, and we said good-bye.

Just as I was leaving, he stopped me. I recall standing outside, holding the screen door open, when Dr. Roberts asked me, "What are you going to be when you get out of the Army?"

I said, "I don't know."

Then he said, "Why don't you do what I do?" I was quite surprised to hear him say that, for it had never occurred to me that I could be like him. After all, I came from a poor family, and none of us had ever completed college, much less become a doctor.

I didn't know what to say. I only replied, "Oh, OK." And then I let the screen door close.

Twenty years later, I was giving a lecture to 200 doctors and scientists at a conference in San Diego. At the end of the lecture, as everyone was filing out of the room, I heard a voice from behind me saying, "The only reason you are here is because of me!" I turned around, and there stood Dr. Jim Roberts! It was the first time I had seen him since I had let that screen door go. As we shook hands, I understood that he was right. I had never started out to be an eye doctor; I'd just wanted to be like him!

I made my career choice based on a person I wanted to emulate, and I have a love of that job, so when I talk to young people in my office, I remind them to look at the adults they know and respect. Sometimes, *who* you will become can be more important than *what* you will become.

Chicago Cop

One of the pleasures of being an eye doctor is that I get to meet people from a great variety of occupations. After seeing tens of thousands of patients, I have come to realize that people with the same occupation have similar traits that are noticeable in an eye examination. Take, for example, law enforcement officers. Policemen have learned to be good decision makers—their lives can depend on it! So when they are in my office and I ask them, "Which is better, one or two," without the slightest hesitation, they will give me a quick, sharp answer.

It is well known that the men and women who do police work develop close relationships and a special bond with their fellow officers. Who could have known that one day, I would be asked to bond with an officer of the law during an eye examination? It all started out as an ordinary day at work, but then...

A patient and I were interrupted by a very sharp knock on the examination room door. I asked the patient to sit back and wait as I slid the microscope off to the side. Opening the door, I saw my receptionist standing there with an odd look of panic on her face. "Is there anything wrong?" I asked.

Speaking softly, she replied, "There is a very large man out at the desk. He's your next patient, but he's very loud and keeps demanding to see you before his examination! He claims that your fee is too high and that he won't pay it! I don't know what to do!"

Now, I'm not a very big guy, but I knew that this was one of those times when the slogan "the buck stops here" applied to me. Walking into the reception area, I was confronted with a well-dressed, gray-haired giant of a man. As expected, he complained bitterly about the cost of my examination. As I was feeling a bit intimidated, and to quiet the guy down, I agreed to cut my fee in half. He then nodded his approval. Shaking my hand, he introduced himself to me as Ken Johnson, and then he quietly took a chair in the waiting room.

When Mr. Johnson sat down in my examination chair, we started by talking about his current position in life. He was retired and had just moved to Eau Claire from Chicago. "What was your occupation?" I asked.

"I was a desk sergeant for the Chicago Police Department," he replied. When I heard that, a light came on in my head! I instantly knew why Mr. Johnson wanted a break on the cost of my services—and it wasn't because he couldn't afford it!

At the end of the examination, I wrapped things up by telling Mr. Johnson that he had healthy eyes and that he needed a new pair of eyeglasses. Standing up, he said, "You can call me Ken, and now I want to take you to lunch."

"Ken," I said, "it's my policy not to socialize with my patients."

A smile came across his face. Crossing his arms over his chest, and blocking the doorway, he responded, "But you did a favor for me. Now you have to let me do a favor for you." Oh, I had known that was coming! You see, in Chicago, the community of police officers socialize with a "you scratch my back and I'll scratch yours" mentality. Allowing someone to return a favor was part of their way of getting along with each other.

So, Ken took me to lunch at Embers, and we had fun. He told me stories about being a Chicago cop, and I told him my stories about being a Chicago bus driver. At the end of lunch, after he paid the bill, he asked me another question: "Do you think you could give my wife an eye exam, too?" Of course, I said that I would be happy to see her. "Well," he went on, "your fee is still too high! Could you do me a favor and cut it in half?" I had a feeling that we would soon be going to lunch together again!

Marked for Life

The world seems to be changing so fast! I suppose that I am getting out of step with many of the new ways, but there are some things that I just don't understand. Tattoos are a good example. The closest that I ever came to getting a tattoo was one night in Juarez, Mexico. I was stationed near there in the Army. My two buddies each came back with an image of a skull across his chest, but I had the good sense to dodge that bullet! Since then, I have seen many young people with all sorts of "body art"! We are certainly not a culture with tribal markings, so I am at a loss to understand the motivation behind permanently altering one's body with a needle and paint. Back in 1982, one of my first Eau Claire patients taught me a lesson that only reinforced my aversion to tattoos—and he was a man of the cloth, no less!

Holding my ophthalmoscope closer to the man's left eye, I noticed some blood vessel changes that suggested problems with his blood pressure. Leaning back, I said, "Sir, would you mind removing your jacket and rolling up your left shirt sleeve? I need to check your blood pressure." Standing up, this tall, somewhat overweight Baptist minister took off his black coat, revealing a long-sleeved white shirt. He began to roll up his right shirtsleeve. "Actually, Pastor, I need to check the left arm instead of the right for a better reading."

He stopped and looked at me with a strange smile on his face. "Well, OK, but I have to warn you that I am embarrassed to show you my left arm. Let me tell you why."

I settled back in my chair to listen to what he had to tell me.

Thirty years ago, before I had even thought about becoming a minister, I enlisted in the Army during the Korean War. You know how it is when you are young; you make decisions that, in hindsight, might not be in your best interest. I felt really tough, and I wanted to get into combat. I was put in a small elite unit, and we were specially trained. After six months in Korea, my platoon had developed a reputation for taking the difficult missions and executing them well. One afternoon, the captain called my squad together. We were told that we were going to parachute behind enemy lines the next day. He expected that this would be a deadly mission and that some of us would not be coming back. That night, a few of us guys decided to go out and have a drink together. I guess you could say that we overdid it a bit, and we ended up in a tattoo parlor! With feelings of solidarity, helped along by a few extra beers, we each stuck out our left arm and got the same tattoo. No matter what would happen the next day, we would all be forever bonded together!

As his story ended, he gingerly pulled up his left sleeve. There, covering his entire upper arm and posing in front of a big red heart, was a nude woman! Adding insult to injury, both the arm and the girl had gotten significantly wider with the passage of time. "I suppose that I should try to have it removed, but I've decided to hide this for the rest of my life. Not the best tattoo for a man of God."

As I fit the blood pressure cuff over his arm, I had to ask, "And Pastor, what happened on the mission?"

He simply shook his head and said, "It was cancelled."

Men Are the Worst Patients!

Men die, on average, seven years earlier than women. Now, I have to tell you that this is not a very comforting thought for me. In fact, it puts me into downright panic mode at times. Even worse, my tendency for a knee-jerk response to facts like this might eventually contribute to my own early (male) demise! Who knows?

But why does my half of the species die so young? Well, I know that modern medicine has applied the best science to answer this question. After decades of study, the conclusion is that *many contributing factors interact in very complex ways.* So now you know! Well, I'm going to do better than that and boil all that research down into one frank and probably honest statement: Men often do things that are stupid. Here are some examples that I've encountered over the years.

First off, imagine I am talking to an elderly man who is losing vision from macular degeneration. I ask him if he is having trouble seeing the Packers on TV, and he immediately responds, "My vision is terrible. I can't even read the score or follow the plays with my eighty-inch TV screen. Can you help me?" Then I ask how well he sees while driving his two-and-a-half-ton truck through heavy traffic at night in a snowstorm, and I get this answer: "No problems at all. I'm seeing just fine. Why do you ask? You're not going to take my driver's license away, are you?"

Now, a woman would have the common sense not to drive a vehicle if she can't see properly. Not a man. I remember another gentleman who caused a serious car accident. When I asked him what happened, he responded, "I don't know. I didn't see a thing." Right there's the first reason men die young!

Here's a second reason: Women never come into my office with bugs in their eyes, but men do. Here's how that conversation goes: "Good morning, sir. I'm Dr. Moritz. What seems to be the problem?"

He then says, "There's a bug in my eye, Doc, and it really hurts." I ask if he's sure it's a bug, and how it happened. He responds, "Oh, it's a bug, alright. I saw it coming straight at me when I was riding my Harley on Interstate 94. Hit me flat in the eye and hurts every time I blink. I think there's still a leg or something in there. This happens a lot."

Well, of course I know the answer to my next question, but I give it a shot anyway: "How did the bug get under your helmet's face shield?"

"Well, Doc, I don't wear my brain bucket unless I need it." Now, how smart can that be? He keeps his helmet handy just in case he's in an accident! Not very bright, but evidently very male!

I had a surgeon once tell me that you can gauge a man's IQ by remembering that it is inversely proportional to the number of pieces of metal he has gotten in his eyes. When I ask such a man about his use of safety glasses, I hear "The metal bounced off the inside of my safety lens and then got into my eye," or "I had safety glasses on all day, but the metal got in after I took them off," or "Wearing safety glasses causes more things to get in my eyes, so I don't wear 'em."

And when does that guy come into my office to have the metal removed? I'll tell you when—it's always Friday afternoon! No guy wants to see a doctor any time, so they delay medical care as long as possible. Then when it's Friday, they realize their weekend is about to be ruined with pain, so suddenly, the problem is a medical emergency!

Guns are another nail in the male coffin. It is common for me to give eye examinations to guys with the complaint "I didn't get my deer this year. I couldn't see the antlers. What's wrong with the glasses that you gave me six years ago?"

Men rarely come into my office *before* the hunt to get a "tune up" on their hunting vision. Now think about this for a moment... Here's a guy who walks around in the woods with a loaded high-powered rifle, not seeing well, and wondering if he is looking at a buck. Or maybe he's looking at another man in his hunting party! Every year, a few more hunters, almost always men, are shot. Just another reason we die young.

A final reason men die young might be because they faint easily. I know this comes as a surprise to you, but nine out of ten people who pass out in my office are male! Here's what I think: Girls use makeup while growing up; most boys don't. Then when it comes time to put in a first contact lens or when the eye doctor has to touch an eye, the guys hit the floor! You might think this is not a flaw, but it can be. The following is a most unusual example.

One day, two men came into my office on an emergency basis. Each had extreme eye pain, and each held a hand over one of his eyes. Apparently, while driving through town, they had had a flat tire. Both had gotten out, taken out the jack, and begun to change the tire. One man inserted the tip of a screwdriver under the edge of the hubcap. As he pried upward, the tip popped out and the sharp screwdriver impaled his left eye! He immediately passed out. Then the other fellow, crouching nearby to help, took one look at this scene and passed out, too—but not before hitting his right eye with the jack handle on the way down!

If it's survival of the fittest, then it's no wonder women live longer than men! Sometimes we are more than just a day late and a dollar short, for we can be downright dangerous to ourselves!

My Most Embarrassing Moment

There is a first time for everything. I remember having a conversation with my cousin Mike many years ago. We had both just gotten out of the Army, and we were talking about our experiences. Mike had been in the Eighty-second Airborne, and he had jumped out of more airplanes than I would have wanted to. I speculated that jumping the first time must have been really scary but that with each subsequent jump, it must have gotten easier. "No, Bert, you've got it backwards," Mike replied. "After the first jump, you realize how crazy parachuting out of an airplane is! Then with each time after that, it just gets more and more terrifying!"

I guess doing something the first time doesn't always go the way we expect. Let me tell you about the first time I gave an eye examination.

It was at the beginning of my third year of optometric training in Chicago. After two years of lectures and lab work, it was finally time for me to give my first eye exam. Dressed in my white clinic coat and proudly carrying my briefcase full of instruments, I went down a long hallway and entered the examination room. There, sitting in the patient chair, was the largest man I had ever seen in my life!

Dressed in full police uniform with service revolver on his hip, gray-haired and distinguished, he stood up to shake my hand. As he reached down and clasped my hand, I wondered if he could feel the clammy sweat on my palm. Looking up at him, I couldn't help but notice that part of his right ear was missing and that knife scars marred his neck! I speculated that these were wounds from years of policing the streets of Chicago. I was in awe of Sergeant O'Leary as I asked him to resume his seat.

I then conducted a series of basic tests, looked inside his eyes to rule out any ocular disease, and checked him for glaucoma. All in all, this was going better than I'd expected. Then it was time to perform a refraction. Little did I know what awaited me.

Refraction is that memorable part of the examination when the doctor asks, "Which is better, one or two?" For a refraction, a very heavy instrument called a Phoroptor, is suspended in front of the patient's eyes. The doctor then attaches a metal rod to the Phoroptor. This rod holds a reading card for measuring bifocal power. As I positioned the Phoroptor in front of Sergeant O'Leary, I reached up and locked the unit tightly into place. Then I attached the rod but forgot to tighten the setscrew that held it in place (a minor error). I proceeded with the test and was confident that I'd found a good correction for his vision.

With the refraction over, it was time to move the Phoroptor away from the patient and to write him a prescription for eyeglasses. I reached up and tried to pull it away. It wouldn't move, not one bit! It seemed to be stuck to the front of his face! I was dumbfounded and felt a sudden sense of panic. I had completely forgotten that all I had to do was unlock the arm as I'd done so many times in class.

What did I do next? In panic, I jerked that instrument as hard as I possibly could. Suddenly, the lock popped loose and the entire thing came flying right at my face! Luckily, just before it hit me, I brought it to a stop. But remember that metal rod that I had failed to lock in place? Well, it flew out and stabbed me dead center in the forehead! Sliding down, it then clipped the tip of my nose and clattered onto the floor. So there I stood, with blood dripping from my forehead and Sergeant O'Leary staring at me! I was bleeding more from my first eye exam than from any of the time I'd spent in the Army! Now, that was really embarrassing!

There is a first time for everything, but sometimes it just doesn't go as expected. After my first eye examination, understandably, I began to worry about the second one! And just like my cousin Mike had suggested, they didn't necessarily get easier with repetition!

ADVENTURES OF A SOUTH DAKOTA KID   211

CPSIA information can be obtained
at www.ICGtesting.com
Printed in the USA
FFOW02n2327130616
24948FF